The Insanity Defense
and
the Trial of
John W. Hinckley, Jr.

THE INSANITY DEFENSE

AND
THE TRIAL OF
JOHN W.
HINCKLEY, JR.

BY
LINCOLN
CAPLAN

DAVID R. GODINE, PUBLISHER, BOSTON

First published in 1984 by
David R. Godine, Publisher, Inc.
306 Dartmouth Street
Boston, Massachusetts 02116

**Library of Congress Cataloging in
Publication Data**
Caplan, Lincoln.
   The insanity defense and the trial of
John W. Hinckley, Jr.
   "Text of this book appeared
originally in The New Yorker in a
somewhat shorter form"—T.p. verso.
   Includes index.
   1. Hinckley, John W.—Trials,
Litigation, etc.   2. Trials
(Assassination)—Washington
(D.C.)   3. Insanity—Jurisprudence—
United States.   4. Criminal liability—
United States.   I. New Yorker (New
York, N.Y.: 1925)   II. Title.
KF224.H56C36   1984
345.73'02524   84-47658
ISBN 0-87923-533-0
347.3052524

The text of this book appeared
originally in *The New Yorker* in a
somewhat shorter form.

Second printing before publication, November 1984

Printed in the United States of America

For Susan

Contents

PROLOGUE — I

I THE OPENING — 7

II M'NAGHTEN'S PROGENY — 19

III CASE HISTORY — 33

IV THE ADAMS TRIAL — 49

V MONEY — 59

VI PSYCHIATRY AND THE LAW — 63

VII THE LAW AND PSYCHIATRY — 75

VIII THE ADAMS CLOSING — 93

IX THE VERDICT — 97

X AFTERMATH — 101

EPILOGUE — 125

ACKNOWLEDGMENTS — 129

INDEX — 131

Prologue

THE VERDICT of not guilty by reason of insanity at the trial of John W. Hinckley, Jr., in 1982, rekindled a controversy that began in England during the middle of the nineteenth century and, in the next hundred years, grew to become the most passionately debated issue in criminal law. The acquittal of the President's would-be assassin once again raised basic questions about the limits of man's responsibility to man. If the workings of the insanity defense were as neat as the phrase itself, both supporters and critics might be justified in posing a stark choice between preserving and limiting, or even abolishing, the legal standard. Instead, under a simple cover, the term holds a thicket of complex subjects about which the facts remain obscure.

The topics range from the dominant one of criminal responsibility, through technical headings like burden of proof and expert testimony in insanity trials, to highly charged issues like the proper disposition of defendants acquitted by reason of insanity. It would be sensible if views on the general subject were based on opinions about the narrower ones within, but this is seldom the case. Even professionals with a stake in the insanity defense, like lawyers, psychiatrists, and mental-health officials, hardly ever break the whole into manageable parts, gather relevant information, and make well-grounded judgments about facets of the legal standard.

Like others, the professionals often cling to beliefs about the insanity defense that rest on intuition, misinformation, or ideology. How often is the defense successful? Who uses it? What happens to offenders if they are acquitted? These are questions few people can answer except with views drawn from sensational anecdotes. In fact, the insanity defense is rarely used and less often successful. Although many insanity defendants are charged with murder, in some states the majority are charged with minor crimes like shoplifting. Even when they are successful (that is to say acquitted), insanity defendants can spend twice as long in hospitals as felons convicted of similar crimes do in prison.

What role does psychiatry play in the defense? What part do jurors play in insanity trials? Many answer these questions incorrectly. In all but a small percentage of insanity acquittals, doctors and lawyers for the prosecution and defense agree on the defendant's mental status, rather than squaring off in debate, and the offender is found not guilty by reason of insanity without a trial. When a defendant is tried, he is more likely to go before a judge as a trier of fact than a jury. What reasons support abolition of the insanity defense? What supports its preservation? The answers rest on basic choices in criminal law.

Professionals, as well as others, often adopt a simplistic way of thinking about the insanity defense that appears to address vexing and immediate concerns. The most pressing concern is the fear of violent crime, with which the defense has been linked in the public mind by cases like John Hinckley's, and the most popular impulse has been to reduce crime by limiting the defense. Even if that impulse could be justified on the grounds that cutting back the legal standard would achieve this goal, the reflex would require choosing between a fundamental American value and a contrary social commitment.

Soon after John Hinckley shot Ronald Reagan and his cohort in 1981, the President's Counselor Edwin Meese took the unusual step of stating as self-evident the proposition that abolishing the insanity defense would rid the streets of dangerous people and reduce violent crime. In debate after the verdict, Attorney General William French Smith took the lead for the Administration, and, expressing a widely held view, posed the alternative of protecting the rights of criminals versus those of society, the forces of law against lawlessness. The Attorney General threw down a daunting—and hyperbolic—choice between liberty and security, between protection of the individual and protection of society.

To guard public safety, Mr. Smith proposed that the government deny individuals the insanity defense, holding offenders accountable even if, because of mental illness, they lacked the ability to tell right from wrong or control their actions. Lumping the sane and the insane in one category, the Attorney General argued that the country should hold blameless only those individuals who lacked the specific intent to do an act on which criminal law rests. Overlooking concerns that a man's free will could be limited by mental illness, so that he would be unable to choose between good and evil as the criminal law now requires, Attorney General Smith, with others, called for a fundamental change in American jurisprudence.

Since the best available information casts doubt on the

idea that limiting the insanity defense will significantly reduce crime, the choice between liberty and security turns
out to be just as misleading. Despite the drama of the Meese
and Smith statements, they, like many others, posed a false
dilemma. By championing a radical shift in a notorious law,
the President's lawyers also diverted attention from monu-
mental problems in the administration of criminal justice.
In a coarse but memorable comment on the distraction,
Professor Alan Stone of Harvard observed: "The insanity
defense may be a pimple on the nose of Justice, but the
patient is dying of congestive heart failure."

The machinery of the insanity defense has many parts
that should improve with tinkering, and the dangers of the
liberty-versus-security dilemma may appear remote in comparison to the benefits of practical reforms. But, as a symbol
of the rise in violent crime, the insanity defense has influence
far beyond its restricted use. Violent crime debases American life. Fear of crime, as Charles Silberman observes in
Criminal Violence, Criminal Justice, is "destroying the net-
work of relationships on which urban and suburban life
depends." Brandished as a symbol, the insanity defense can
arouse this fear of crime and move citizens to support far-
reaching actions.

In the extreme, the standard can persuade citizens to give
up legal safeguards on the grounds that the new order will
increase protection for society. In crime bills passed by the
United States Senate in 1984, and heralded under the ban-
ner of limits on the insanity defense, this trade-off was implicit in provisions denying bail to dangerous but un-
convicted defendants, who are locked up before trial, and
in limits on the exclusionary rule permitting the government
to present illegally obtained evidence at trial. Even when
there is value gained for value given, the erosion of liberty
for the sake of security threatens fundamental principles.

When the trade-off is false, as becomes evident in a careful study of the insanity defense, and the law gives up safeguards without any assurance of improvement in public safety, the government takes a step toward tyranny.

CHAPTER ONE

The
Opening

THE TRIAL OF John W. Hinckley, Jr., opened in May, 1982, in Washington, D.C., with a videotape that stilled the federal courtroom. Six color television sets on carts of various heights were angled to face the jury, gallery, and counsels' tables, and a small screen faced Judge Barrington Parker on his bench. At the judge's direction, the monitors snapped on to show a tape made in Dayton, Ohio, during a 1980 Presidential campaign trip. President Jimmy Carter's limousine arrived at the Dayton convention center on a bright October day, and the President emerged with a stiff wave and smile, and plunged into the crowd, grabbing hands. Then the crowd noise faded and the courtroom was silent. The videotape inched along in stop action and, in front of a monitor, the cameraman who had taken the footage used a pointer to direct the eyes of the jurors to the upper-right quadrant of the screen, where half of Hinckley's face—his nose, his eyes, a wave of hair across his forehead —was visible behind frozen arms and faces. The meaning of the tape was clear: at least six months before he shot

Ronald Reagan and three others on March 30th, 1981, Hinckley was what the prosecutor called "a hunter and a stalker."

A tape of the March 30th shooting, familiar from repeated showings on television soon after the event, played in the courtroom like an anticlimax, but its impact lingered. As his tape suggested, the cameraman had stood a few feet from Hinckley in the mist outside the Washington Hilton, shortly before two-thirty in the afternoon, and he had recorded the young man's arm and hand as Hinckley aimed at President Reagan. On the courtroom screens, the President moved quickly from right to left, surrounded by aides and protectors. Above the noise of the jostling crowd, a voice yelled, "President Reagan, President Reagan!" The President turned toward the camera, and six shots sounded, a swift sequence of pops that were muffled by city traffic. The attack was over in seconds. A Secret Service agent testified about reaching Hinckley after the shooting: "As I was going through the air, I can still remember the gun going off and a desperate feeling of 'I have got to get to it. I have to get to it and stop it.' " He continued, "I came down on top of the assailant, with my right arm around his head. . . . He was still clicking the weapon as we go down."

The government's senior prosecutor was Roger Adelman, a tall and commanding veteran with a boyish haircut and the eyes of an owl in a hawk's face. He wore G-man suits with wide lapels, and broad ties in stars and stripes to match. In his opening statement of the government's case, Adelman demonstrated how Hinckley had crouched like a marksman to aim his twenty-two-caliber pistol and clear a path to the President. Hinckley's first shot hit press secretary James Brady in the face, piercing to the brain. His second shot struck policeman Thomas Delahanty in the back. The third went over the President's head and landed in a building across the street. Hinckley moved from left to right, and his fourth shot, aimed at Reagan, caught Secret Service agent Timothy McCarthy in the chest. Still moving, Hinckley fired a fifth shot and hit the bullet-proof glass of the President's limousine. The sixth shot ricocheted off the rear panel of the car, entered the President's chest, glanced off a rib, and lodged in a lung, inches from his heart. Adelman counted out loud—"With six shots, Mr. Hinckley hit four people"—and declared that these were "the central and critical events" of the case.

While Adelman described the shooting, John Hinckley sat at counsel's table and stared into the middle distance, blinking rapidly. From the first day of jury selection, when Hinckley stood before a roomful of potential jurors and the judge asked if any of them knew the defendant, it was tempting to watch him all the time, especially at moments when his snits and posturings might seem telling. His insanity defense turned the trial into a mystery, and Hinckley sat on stage for all to inspect for clues. He looked smaller than life, dwarfed by the high ceilings and windowless walls of the sixth-floor courtroom. The room's neutral tones drained him of color. Facing the jury, Hinckley sat slump-shouldered, surrounded by three burly marshals within arm's length, with a half-dozen others at the doors of the courtroom. He was pale and moon-faced, his skin scarred by acne. The collar of his white shirt and his brown tie hung loose at his neck, and his tan suit, which he alternated with a blue blazer and gray slacks, was too big. He appeared younger than his twenty-seven years, and the lawyers and witnesses often referred to him as John. He folded his hands on the table, twiddled his thumbs, tapped them together, then carefully wiped his glasses. When not lost in thought, rubbing his forehead with both hands, he was visibly bored, wary, or faintly amused, smiling out of the side of his mouth. When he glanced at the gallery, his eyes rolled to the tops of their sockets and, against fields of white, his pupils were small, dark, and opaque.

The senior attorney for the defense was Vincent Fuller, a partner of Edward Bennett Williams in the Washington law firm of Williams & Connolly. Fuller was short and stocky, with slick, silver hair and a thick voice on which he sometimes choked. In the opening argument for the defense, he told a bizarre, compelling story. By 1976, when Hinckley was twenty-one, fantasies had become the "driving force" in his life: he was going to become "a great musical talent." He went to Hollywood to sell his songs, failed, and "happened upon" the movie *Taxi Driver*. Hinckley saw the movie "as many as fifteen times" and it "remained" with him. He began to take on traits of Travis Bickle, the movie's protagonist, a loner who turns from political assassination to the rescue of a young prostitute named Iris. Jodie Foster played Iris in the film, and in the spring of 1980 Hinckley read in *People* magazine that she was going to Yale University in the fall. She became his obsession. He visited New Haven, and when he failed to interest her he retreated "into this world of isolation." He bought guns, stalked Presidents Carter and Reagan, and was "devastated" by the death of John Lennon. For five months—from October, 1980, through February, 1981—Hinckley saw Dr. John Hopper, a psychiatrist in Evergreen, Colorado, where his parents lived, and, in an autobiography he wrote for the doctor, described his feelings about Jodie Foster. The psychiatrist didn't probe these delusions and, instead, recommended on January 23rd that Hinckley's parents give him a deadline: by March 1st, he was to have a job; by the end of March, with a job or not, he was to be out of the house and on his own. On March 25th, Hinckley flew to Hollywood, realized again he'd have no success in music, and took a bus cross-country, intending to reach New Haven via Washington, D.C. On March 29th he checked into a Washington hotel, and on March 30th he chanced on a local newspaper with the President's schedule. In a neat script, on white, lined notebook paper, he wrote a letter, which he left in his hotel room:

3/30/81

12:45 P.M.

Dear Jodie,

There is a definite possibility that I will be killed in my attempt to get Reagan. It is for this very reason that I am writing you this letter now.

As you well know by now I love you very much. Over the past seven months I've left you dozens of poems, letters and love messages in the faint hope that you could develop an interest in me. Although we talked on the phone a couple of times I never had the nerve to simply approach you and introduce myself. Besides my shyness, I honestly did not wish to bother you with my constant presence. I know the many messages left at your door and in your mailbox were a nuisance, but I felt that it was the most painless way for me to express my love for you.

I feel very good about the fact that you at least know my name and know how I feel about you. And by hanging around your dormitory, I've come to realize that I'm the topic of more than a little conversation, however full of ridicule it may be. At least you know that I'll always love you.

Jodie, I would abandon this idea of getting Reagan in a second if I could only win your heart and live out the rest of my life with you, whether it be in total obscurity or whatever.

I will admit to you that the reason I'm going ahead with this attempt now is because I just cannot wait any longer to impress you. I've got to do something now to make you understand, in no uncertain terms, that I am doing all of this for your sake! By sacrificing my freedom and possibly my life, I hope to change your mind about me. This letter is being written only an hour before I leave for the Hilton Hotel. Jodie, I'm asking you to please look into your heart and at least give me the chance, with this historical deed, to gain your respect and love.

I love you forever,

John Hinckley

As the bailiff announced him each morning, Judge Parker entered the courtroom and, against a backdrop of dark marble on the center wall and blond wood paneling on the others, he lifted himself slowly up the steps to the bench. He used crutches because he had lost a leg when a car hit him as he crossed a Washington street. Besides an occasional cough, the only sounds were the solemn thump of crutches on wood and the satin rustle of people rising to attention. From his high perch, the judge surveyed the room with a cool eye and a large, grave face. A black Republican who was appointed to the federal district bench by President Richard Nixon, Parker had already contributed a stirring footnote to history. In 1977, he presided over the trial of former Director of Central Intelligence Richard Helms. When Helms pleaded no contest to charges of failing to tell Congress the truth about the C.I.A.'s role in the overthrow of Chilean President Salvador Allende Gossens, Parker gave him a suspended sentence of two years and a fine of two thousand dollars. He also pronounced Helms "in disgrace and shame," and sternly declared, "From this day forward, let there be no doubt: No one, whatever his position in or out of government, is above the law."

After the prosecution's first round of witnesses, including a motel maid who described Hinckley as "a normal All-American-type boy" and a ballistics expert who traced the history of Hinckley's guns, the defendant's parents cast an emotional spell. JoAnn Moore Hinckley, John's mother, was the first witness for the defense. She wore a salmon-pink outfit, with Peter Pan collar and bow, and spoke in a soft Texas accent. The month before the March shooting was the worst in her memory. On March 1st, John left a note, which she recited: "Dear Mom and Dad, Your prodigal son has left again to exorcise some demons." On March 6th, before dawn, he called from New York City in "a bad state." His parents asked him to compose himself and call back. In the meantime, they called Dr. Hopper, John's psychiatrist. "Give John a hundred dollars and tell him good-bye," was Hopper's advice. A day later, John returned to Colorado, but his parents did not let him come home. On March 25th—"I remember it was a Wednesday"—JoAnn Hinckley drove John from his motel to the airport. "It was so hard to see John go, because I felt in my mind that once again John might be leaving and maybe he might try to take his own life. . . . We didn't say one word to each other all the way down to the airport." She continued, "I broke the plan for the first time, and I gave him some money of my own. . . . He looked so bad, and so sad, and so absolutely in total despair and I was frightened, and I didn't know what he was going to do, but yet I kept thinking, I've got to stick to that plan." At the airport, "John got out of the car and I couldn't even look at him. And he said, 'Well, Mom, I want to thank you for everything. I want to thank you for everything you have ever done for me.' " JoAnn Hinckley went on, "And I said, 'Well, you are very welcome.' And I said it so coldly because I didn't want him to know what I was thinking."

The face of John W. Hinckley, Sr., showed marks of strength—a smooth, domed forehead, ruddy cheeks, arched and skeptical brows—but his voice barely hid his distress. He confirmed differences between himself and John—"He wasn't going to stay at home and do nothing," or "I was upset when he told us that he had written a novel"—and his blunt talk earned him trust from the gallery. Against the psychiatrist's initial advice, Jack Hinckley had arranged for John to fly from Newark to Denver on March 7th. On the way to the airport that Saturday night, he prayed that he and his wife were doing the right thing. Looking "dazed, wiped out," John entered the terminal and Jack took him aside. He testified: "I told him how disappointed I was in him, how he had let us down, and how he had not followed the plan that we had all agreed on. And that he had just left us no choice but to not take him back to the house again, but to force him to go on his own. And so that's what I did. I took him to his car which was parked at the airport. It was an old car and the radiator leaked. And I put some antifreeze in it and we got the car started. And I had a couple of hundred dollars with me that I had brought from the house. And I gave that to him and I suggested that he go to the Y.M.C.A., and he said, No, he didn't want to do that. And so I said, 'O.K., you are on your own. Do whatever you want to.' "

JoAnn Hinckley sobbed on a gallery bench. As one of her son's lawyers scurried to her side, she leaned forward and covered her eyes with a small, pink handkerchief. Her husband continued, in a low voice: "In looking back on that, I'm sure that was the greatest mistake in my life. I am the cause of John's tragedy. We forced him out at a time that he just simply couldn't cope. I wish to God that I could trade places with him right now." As JoAnn left the courtroom, Jack brought a folded handkerchief to his face. His eyes were hidden by the rectangle of cloth, and his shoulders heaved as he sat on the witness stand.

During his mother's testimony, John shielded his eyes and bent over the table. While his father talked, John drummed his fingers, flushed, and stared into space. His brother and sister provoked other signs of feeling. When his twenty-nine-year-old sister Diane came into the courtroom, he gave her a limp but sincere wave. When Scott, who was thirty-one and ran the family oil and gas business, mentioned his hope that John would prosper as a popular musician—perhaps as the next Barry Manilow—John shook his head, apparently embarrassed and bemused.

Besides Hinckley's own behavior, testimony from two dozen witnesses gave some grounds for speculation about his mind and character during the first weeks of the trial. A videotape of Jodie Foster's testimony provided more to go on. The tape was made on the first anniversary of the shooting, in March, 1982, during a special session held secretly to protect Miss Foster from the glare of trial, and was shown after Jack Hinckley's stint on the stand. The television sets were moved back into position and Miss Foster filled the screens. She appeared plain and unexciting. Her girlish alto lacked verve, and her long blond hair kept drifting across her face. During the showing, John turned his chair toward the closest screen, carefully put on his glasses, and watched the tape like a faithful hound, looking up as he cradled his head on his hands. He smiled when Jodie Foster was asked the date she first heard from him by phone. "I can give you a reference," she volunteered, citing a new-wave event. "It was the weekend of a Pretenders' concert."

Toward the end of the tape, John shifted and strained at his collar. Jodie Foster was asked to look at the defendant, who had sat across the courtroom from her, and tell the court if she had ever seen him before. In real life, John's eyes swept away from the screen in a quick, wounded glance at the gallery, and he motioned for the marshals to escort him from the room. The jury took minor note of Hinckley's departure, rocking attentively before their two screens, and, on tape, Jodie Foster took the next question. "How would you describe your relationship with John

Hinckley?" she was asked. "I don't have any relationship with John Hinckley," she answered. The jury did not see the whole tape of Jodie Foster—did not see Hinckley throw a pen at her (it hit her lawyer), or, after she ignored him at the taping, hear him threaten to kill her.

The media bazaar continued the next morning. The judge ordered the marshals to give each member of the jury a pair of headphones, after which they listened to three audio tapes that were also played through speakers—the first time John Hinckley's voice filled the courtroom. Over the crackle of static, his voice was high, sweet, and nasal. Hinckley made the first tape in New Haven, when he telephoned Jodie Foster's room at Yale, in September of 1980. When he finally reached her, he tacked between polite answers and eager questions, maneuvering to keep her on the line. Unguarded, her voice on the telephone perked in comparison to the drone of her videotape. She protested mildly, pulled between curiosity about the boy on the line and the instinct that she should hang up on him. Behind signs of the coquette, she also displayed the firm tact of an actress who is used to letting boys down gently.

The second tape contained a recording that Hinckley had made of himself playing the guitar and singing ballads. One was a song written by John Lennon for his wife, Yoko Ono. Hinckley substituted Jodie's name for Yoko's and, to a basic strum, he sang:

> In the middle of the night,
> In the middle of the night I call your name.
> Oh, Jodie,
> Oh, Jodie,
> My love will turn you on.

The guitar strayed off key, but Hinckley's voice touched each note in a breathy, clear, and pleasant tenor, with almost no vibrato. The walls of the courtroom seemed to move in closer. The songs were meant as solos in rooms for one, behind a shut door. The third tape, addressed to himself, contained Hinckley's New Year's message "for the end of 1980 coming upon 1981," a lugubrious, self-conscious rambling, filled with clichés, threats, prissy stand-ins for obscenities, and dull comments on personal matters. He maundered about John Lennon and Jodie Foster, insanity and suicide, and always about himself. The monologue revealed Hinckley as miserable, sad, and wanting.

CHAPTER TWO

M'Naghten's Progeny

SINCE THE nineteenth century, the insanity defense has periodically burst on the criminal law, like Halley's comet, and then disappeared until a celebrated case, such as John Hinckley's, made it shine again. The most famous case in the history of the defense occurred in England in 1843. Daniel M'Naghten was a Scottish woodcutter who suffered from the delusion that he was persecuted by the Pope, the Jesuits, and Prime Minister Robert Peel. He set out to shoot Sir Robert but, by mistake, shot Peel's secretary, Edward Drummond, instead. Nine medical experts testified for the defense, and the prosecution offered none in rebuttal. To public outrage, M'Naghten was found not guilty by reason of insanity.

A popular verse admonished: "Ye people of England: exult and be glad/For you're now at the will of the merciless mad." Queen Victoria, addressing Parliament, joined the public in disapproving of the verdict. M'Naghten's was the fifth attempt on a prime minister's or sovereign's life since the turn of the century, including several on the Queen's, and she feared the acquittal would goad cranks and radicals to try to kill her. To account for the apparent miscarriage of justice in M'Naghten's case, the fifteen ranking common-law judges were asked by the House of Lords to answer basic questions about the insanity defense. With one dissenter, they stated the law passed down from twelfth-century canon law, and practiced by Henry III, who, in the thirteenth century, had pardoned murderers of unsound mind. The king's acts of grace anticipated the first recorded insanity verdict by a jury, in 1505. The answers of the judges, three centuries later, filled the report of Lord Chief Justice Tindal, who also presided at M'Naghten's trial.

The response to one query became known as the M'Naghten rule, which held that a man is not responsible for his criminal acts when, because of a "disease of the mind," he does not know the "nature and quality" of his acts or does not know they are "wrong." The rule fixed in law a principle of justice that can be read into Biblical chapters beginning with Genesis 2, verse 9, about good and evil, into Talmudic records of Jewish law about special treatment for deaf-mutes, idiots, and minors who injure someone without intent, into Greek philosophy and Roman law: society should not hold a man criminally responsible or morally blameworthy for unlawful acts he commits because he lacks the capacity to tell right from wrong.

The most celebrated case in the American history of the defense—until Hinckley's—took place in Washington, D.C., in 1881, and confirmed M'Naghten as the rule of law in the District of Columbia until the middle of the twentieth century. At the capital's railroad station, a sometime religious fanatic and would-be consul named Charles Guiteau took out a British bulldog pistol and shot President James Garfield. After the President's death, the trial of the odd and changeable Guiteau turned into a two-month spectacle. The defendant read the *New York Herald* and the *Washington Post* in court, and often leaped up to express aloud his prejudices, including his contempt for "poodle dogs in the newspaper business." On cross-examination, he scolded the prosecutor, "I do not care a snap for your fierce look. Just cool right down." When a neurologist claimed under oath that one out of every five Americans was insane, the prosecutor responded, "That is a liberal and most encouraging prospect for all of us." Guiteau was convicted and hanged, despite testimony about his "insane delusion" that God had instructed him "to remove the President for the good of the American people." "My free agency was destroyed," he declared. "I had to do it. That's all there is about it."

In 1954, Judge David Bazelon of the United States Court of Appeals for the District of Columbia issued an opinion that adopted and established a test first stated by the New Hampshire Supreme Court in the late nineteenth century. Called the Durham rule, the standard quickly became more famous than the facts that prompted it. Monte Durham had been convicted of housebreaking, after a long history of mental problems, petty crime, and time spent in and out of various hospitals and prisons. In its first opinion on his case, the Court of Appeals reversed Monte's conviction for housebreaking and directed the lower court to try the case again under the Durham rule, which it had just articulated. When the defendant was convicted once more, the appeals court overturned that ruling, too. The third time around, the trial court reached the verdict the appellate bench seemed to want all along—not guilty by reason of insanity. For the appeals court, Judge Bazelon wrote that an "accused is not criminally responsible if his unlawful act was the product of mental disease or mental defect." Judge Bazelon's simple test attempted to solve problems that had been debated since Guiteau's trial, almost three-quarters of a century before. A man could know right from wrong and either lack emotional appreciation that what he did was wrong or lack control because of his derangement. Under M'Naghten's "right-wrong" standard, he could still be convicted; under Durham's "product" test, he could be acquitted.

The Durham rule also addressed a problem that had arisen in Washington in another case, in 1929, when the "irresistible impulse," or "volitional," test supplemented the "cognitive" standard of M'Naghten. First set forth by an American court in 1834, the test provided a defense for a man whose mental illness caused him to lose self-control. The concept grew from the pioneering ideas of the American forensic psychiatrist Isaac Ray, whose "Medical Jurisprudence of Insanity" provided evidence at M'Naghten's trial. Under the new Durham rule, a man could be acquitted if his acts resulted from brooding and reflection, and not just from a momentary seizure. The old criterion, fashioned when physicians of the mind were called alienists, did not "take sufficient account of psychic realities," Judge Bazelon explained: "Durham was designed to throw open the windows of the defense and ventilate a musty doctrine with all of the information acquired during a century's study of the intricacies of human behavior." The rule allowed psychiatrists to testify about all evidence on a defendant's mental condition, not just about his ability to tell right from wrong. The rule also shifted the burden of proof in insanity cases: under M'Naghten, a defendant had to raise the issue of and prove his insanity; under Durham, the defendant still had to raise the defense, but, once he raised it, the prosecution had to prove him sane beyond a reasonable doubt.

In the decade after Durham, the District of Columbia became a laboratory for the insanity defense. Durham had stirred old questions: What was mental disease? Was there a link between a particular disease and crime? Even Judge

Bazelon's allies had second thoughts about the ruling, which left to psychiatrists and juries the task of answering these questions. The percentage of successful insanity pleas in Washington cases jumped from less than one-half of one percent in 1954 to over fourteen percent in 1961, although the increase may have been due in part to acquittals of defendants who had previously been held incompetent to stand trial. But, as a proportion of all criminal cases in the District, insanity acquittals remained small. They went from almost six to twenty-five per thousand cases. Judge Bazelon later wrote that "Durham actually produced very little change at all," but an elaborate jury study proved that the new insanity law made a difference. As part of a project at the University of Chicago, Rita James Simon presented facts from a housebreaking or incest case to 1176 jurors in Chicago, Minneapolis, and St. Louis. Deliberating in panels about one of the fact patterns, the jurors reached different verdicts if they applied the M'Naghten test, the Durham rule, or personal standards, and found that decisions made under the new law came closest to their personal sense of justice.

Thirty state and five federal courts reviewed the Durham rule in the decade that followed. Because it gave judges and juries no practical guidance, all of the courts rejected the new law. Only two states, Vermont and Maine, adopted the law by statute. The Supreme Court touched on the standard, but, declining to pass judgment, used the controversy about the Durham rule to make another point: "It is simply not yet the time to write into the Constitution formulas cast in terms whose meaning, let alone relevance, is not yet clear either to doctors or to lawyers." In 1972, after scores of opinions in which District judges sharpened the terms of the Durham rule by addressing the scope of expert testimony, instructions of the judge to the jury, and even the definition of mental disease or defect at the heart of the law's test of insanity, the Court of Appeals for the District abandoned it altogether and settled on the current Brawner rule. In Brawner, the judges adopted a model test of the American Law Institute that followed the approach of a British Royal Commission on Capital Punishment published in 1953 and soon became the law in the majority of states.

Archie Brawner killed a man, firing his gun through a hallway door. He had been drinking wine all day and then had gone to a party. His jaw was injured in a fight there and, in a rage, Brawner left, picked up the gun, and returned for vengeance. After the fight, a witness said, "He looked like he was out of his mind," and experts for both sides at trial testified that Archie suffered from a psychiatric or neurological problem. Brawner was acquitted on that basis. The Brawner rule articulated by the court held that a man is not responsible if, as a result of mental disease or defect, he "lacks substantial capacity to appreciate the wrongfulness of his conduct or to conform his conduct to the requirements of the law." The test replaced knowledge with appreciation, so a defendant could be acquitted if he knew right from wrong but his thinking was severely disordered and he lacked emotional appreciation of the difference. The test also expanded the notion of "irresistible impulse," getting at the concept of self-control through the more general word "conform" in the second part of the standard. To make it hard for people with antisocial personalities to use the defense successfully—people whose disorders showed only by repeated criminal or antisocial behavior—the test included a section known as the caveat paragraph, which stated that the terms "mental disease or defect" did not include these sociopaths.

The Brawner rule did not end controversy about the insanity defense. In the period of revisionist thinking sparked by the Durham ruling—roughly since 1960—debate about the defense stretched to include far more than discussion of mental illness and criminal law, and it continues today. According to the F.B.I.'s 1982 Index of Crime, the annual number of crimes in the United States since 1960 has swelled by almost four hundred percent, to near thirteen million. The crime rate per capita has tripled and the rate of violent crime has risen even higher. A chilling symbol of this growth is the rise in the number of killers who strike repeatedly, in serial murders. According to the Justice Department, between 1978 and 1983, there were at least seventeen men who killed ten or more people each; including the five previous years, there were thirty. Although the National Crime Survey, available only since 1973, suggests that the F.B.I.'s absolute figures are too low and its rate of increase too high, and critics question the Bureau's methods of gathering facts, no one disputes the increase over time. Abraham Goldstein, a Yale Law School professor and a former clerk to Judge Bazelon, wrote several years ago, "Because the currents calling criminal responsibility into question are so strong, those who look to the criminal law to shore up weakened social supports see the insanity defense as a call to battle."

If the defense is a challenge, it should seldom be heard. According to a recent study, in 1978—the last year for which national data are available on the insanity defense—almost a third of American households were touched by crime, and forty million people were victims; ten million suspects were arrested, and about three-fifths of the presumed offenders were charged; approximately two-thirds of these pleaded guilty. 1,625 of the defendants successfully pleaded insanity—less than one-tenth of one percent of the presumed offenders who stood trial.

Dr. Alan Stone, a professor at Harvard's law and medical

schools, observed recently in a paper for the American Psychiatric Association that the insanity defense changed markedly in the post-Durham period. Before 1954, in his view, the defense had been "a profound hypocrisy." Courts found defendants not guilty by reason of insanity and then confined them for the rest of their lives in institutions for the criminally insane "more awful than prisons." The law helped lift the veil of hypocrisy, in a series of decisions that rejected the automatic and indefinite confinement of these defendants. Legal reforms gave them rights to new hearings after trial, to determine whether they were still mentally ill and dangerous. If committed, they were entitled to periodic review of their status. Psychiatry also lent a hand. Until the 1950s, long-term confinement of the mentally ill was an accepted practice; then, Stone said in his paper, psychiatrists "finally opened their eyes to the evils of long-term institutionalization." They also discovered effective drug treatments and began to favor community mental-health care. Hospital stays dropped from years to days, in cases where questions about therapy, as opposed to punishment, were the only ones that had to be answered. In 1955, in Illinois, for example, there were forty-eight thousand beds for mental patients in state hospitals, who spent an average of ten years and eight months there. In 1982, there were ten thousand beds in the state, half of them for the severely retarded, and the average stay for someone mentally ill was twenty-two days. After Durham, a mentally-ill offender had to be restored to competency before he could be tried and plead insanity; before facing judgment about his responsibility in the past, he had to prove his current ability to understand charges against him in court. Stone advised, "From the psychiatrist's current perspective, almost everyone who has had sufficient treatment to be restored to competency has had as much in-hospital treatment as is necessary for therapeutic reasons."

Hospitals still keep defendants found not guilty by reason of insanity for an average of two to three and a half years (in Washington, D.C., the average is over five years, with those charged with felonies staying about a year longer than those charged with misdemeanors), but as the consequences of a successful insanity plea have changed, the defense has become more attractive. There is evidence that the absolute number of insanity acquittals has increased. In New York, for example, between 1965 and 1971, an average of eight acquittals occurred each year. In 1972, that number tripled, and by 1975 there were sixty-one acquittals. Between September, 1980, and December, 1983, following passage of the state's Insanity Defense Reform Act, designed to limit use of the defense, there were three hundred and forty acquittals—an average of about a hundred a year. These numbers should not be presented out of context; of all those arrested in New York, less than one-half of one percent avoid the criminal justice system for mental-health reasons like incompetence, and less than two percent of this tiny portion successfully plead insanity. But the fraction is on the rise. "Perhaps for the first time in history," Stone declared in 1982, "a successful plea of insanity has real bite."

Like many other scholars, Stone has measured the social impact of the defense. The issue that seems to concern observers most deeply is what happens to a defendant after a successful plea, especially if he has committed a violent act; predictions as to further violent behavior have been called "the greatest unresolved problem the criminal justice system faces" by Milton Rector, when he was president of the National Council on Crime and Delinquency. A handful of surgeons perform controversial brain operations to control violent behavior, but, as Stone emphasized, "Psychiatry certainly has not found a permanent cure for violence." In his view, giving rights to the mentally ill also means enduring risks of injury by them. So does releasing successful insanity defendants, even after treatment. Statistics on recidivism in the mentally ill are inconclusive. A study by John Monahan, of the University of Virginia, declares that the best predictions concerning the likelihood of danger from individual ex-inmates are wrong two out of three times, erring most often by forecasting that ex-inmates will do violence that they in fact avoid. Another report, by Monahan and Henry Steadman, of New York's Office of Mental Health, emphasizes that the probability of repeated crime by a mentally-ill offender in the state is somewhat lower than for a felon released from prison. In other words, there is less reason to fear repeated crimes by a mentally-ill offender than by a felon, no matter what the individual prediction may be.

As Dr. Stone asserted, the purpose of the insanity defense is to "insure that the criminal law has moral authority." For his definition of authority, he cited the Brawner decision. "The concept of 'belief in freedom of the human will and a consequent ability and duty of the normal individual to choose between good and evil' is a core concept that is 'universal and persistent in mature systems of law,' " the court said at the time, continuing, "Criminal responsibility is assessed when through 'free will' a man elects to do evil. . . . The concept of lack of 'free will' is both the root of origin of the insanity defense and the line of its growth." Put more simply, the insanity defense should be the exception that proves the rule. The few who are found not guilty by reason of insanity assure that the rest of society can be held accountable under the law.

Abraham Goldstein, the Yale Law School professor who wrote a definitive text, *The Insanity Defense,* agreed with

Stone's analysis, but made a point that moved the discussion from theory to practice. "The real problem," he declared, "has been to find a formula that keeps the exemption closely attuned to what the public can accept." It is important to draw a line between madness and badness, so to speak, but it is difficult to keep the line from moving. As England's Lord Devlin, one of the country's distinguished jurists, observed, "the concept of illness expands continually at the expense of the concept of moral responsibility."

Others have called for outright abolition of the insanity defense. Norval Morris, a professor at the University of Chicago Law School, called the defense "a genuflection to a deep-seated moral sense that the mentally ill lack freedom of choice to do good or ill and that therefore blame should not be imputed to them for their otherwise criminal acts nor punishment imposed." He considered the defense a piece of hypocrisy. Despite Judge Bazelon's statement that "our collective conscience does not allow punishment where it cannot impose blame," the insanity defense draws an arbitrary line between psychological and social adversity, and other pressures on human behavior. Why one, without the others? asked Morris. (Bazelon agreed, and would allow evidence about racial and economic hardship, as well as psychology and medicine, in insanity trials, though this view has never had the force of law.) More important, Morris felt, the defense is "morally false" because it does not apply to all defendants who need psychiatric treatment, nor to those who are already in prison and need it most. According to him, the insanity defense has become an "ornate rarity," but also a "moral outrage," because a small number of mentally-ill offenders invoke it, while the vast majority are convicted and punished, and few of their disorders are really treated.

To redress the balance of fairness, Morris recommended that the question of insanity be considered, in a standard criminal trial, only as far as it bears on the defendant's intent—called in legal language *mens rea,* and translated as "guilty mind"—to commit the physical act. A man who believed he was squeezing a lemon when he strangled his wife, for example, could be found not guilty because he lacked the intent to choke her. In a variation of the *mens rea* test, the man might have known what he was doing but, because he was deranged, lacked a specific intent to strangle his wife. He could have meant to shake her but, because of his mental condition, failed to realize that his vigorous hold would kill. Under the doctrine of diminished capacity, he could be convicted of a lesser charge than murder, such as manslaughter. After conviction, Morris suggested, a defendant's mental illness should determine whether he is sent to a hospital or a prison. His illness at the time of the crime should be taken into account to reduce the severity of punishment, and the likelihood of his future violence should be taken into account to increase punishment. Chief Justice Warren Burger, then a federal appeals judge, endorsed this approach at a conference of state trial judges in 1963. Norval Morris pushed for a definition of insanity that went back almost a century and a half. Contrary to the principle at the heart of the insanity defense, Morris argued for more stringent treatment of all mentally-ill offenders. He claimed that they deserve no more favor than alcoholics, ghetto blacks, or defendants who are victims of hard times.

Doubts about fairness open the insanity defense to other attacks—as a privilege of the rich, for example, or as a tool of oppression against the poor. Some psychologists also argue that the idea of man as a responsible agent with free will is wrong and is, therefore, a misleading foundation for support of the insanity defense. They present the behaviorists' view, which assumes that free will is an illusion, that blame cannot be assigned for behavior conditioned by forces beyond the power of the individual, and that the system of justice should either change—through psychosurgery, drugs, or therapy—the personalities of people who commit antisocial acts, or, if change proves impossible, confine them. According to this theory, there is no basis or need for an insanity defense.

Until 1982, debate on the insanity defense quickened only by the irregular appearance of defendants in sensational cases. In 1924, in the case that assured his fame, sixty-seven-year-old Clarence Darrow defended Richard Loeb and Nathan Leopold, Jr., the young, rich Chicagoans who confessed to the kidnapping and murder of another son of privilege in a failed attempt at the perfect crime. To the public's surprise, the teenagers pleaded guilty. Raising the insanity defense for scrutiny if not for the court's consideration, Darrow presented evidence of the young men's mental disease "in mitigation of the punishment." "ROPE WILL NOT CURE CRIME, DARROW SAYS IN PLEA FOR SLAYERS," the *Chicago Daily News* reported in a headline. In a three-day summary after the month-long trial, Darrow persuaded the judge not to sentence the young men to hanging. Instead they were dispatched to a life of prison, where Loeb was stabbed to death and Leopold set up an educational system for inmates. From 1835—when Richard Lawrence accosted President Andrew Jackson at point-blank range in the rotunda of the United States Capitol, with pistols that misfired, and a jury took five minutes to return a verdict of not guilty by reason of insanity before sending Lawrence to confinement for life—until 1982, with odd exceptions like the insanity acquittal of the saloonkeeper who shot Teddy Roosevelt in the chest in 1912, the infamous defendants have been convicted. The attackers of Robert Kennedy,

Martin Luther King, Jr., John Lennon, Gerald Ford, and George Wallace were none of them acquitted by reason of insanity. Most successful insanity defendants have been anonymous young men, although the weirdest defendants (the agents of Satan or vampire killers) sometimes achieve notoriety. John Hinckley broke the string, kindling a new trial of the insanity defense.

CHAPTER THREE

Case
History

IN THE HINCKLEY TRIAL, neither side presented an un-interrupted biography or even a simple chronicle of the defendant's life. The story came out in awkward, repetitive bits, through the questions and answers of lawyers and witnesses. John Hinckley was born in Ardmore, Oklahoma, in 1955. When he was four, his family moved to Dallas, where John quarterbacked his elementary-school football team, starred in basketball, and, at nine, became a Beatles fan when the group toured the United States. In the sixth grade, John moved with his family to the suburb of Highland Park, a fine neighborhood and home to many prominent Texans. The Hinckleys' house had a swimming pool in the back yard and a private Coke machine. According to his mother, John was no longer "kingpin." He began to play the guitar, and in junior high he managed the football team. ("He had his own little withdrawn personality, and that was fine," his mother said.) In 1973, after he graduated from high school, the family moved to Evergreen, Colorado—near Denver—where Jack Hinckley established a new headquarters for the family business, the Vanderbilt Energy Corporation. John enrolled at Texas Tech, in Lubbock. He finished his freshman year, and in the summer of 1974 moved to Dallas, living first with Diane, her husband, Steve Sims, and their son Chris, and then later on his own. In the autobiography composed for psychiatrist John Hopper he wrote: "I stayed by myself in my apartment and dreamed of future glory in some undefined field, perhaps music or politics."

In 1975, he returned to Lubbock for the spring semester at Texas Tech, where he was assigned a black roommate. "My naive, race-mixed ideology was forever laid to rest," he later scrawled in an essay about his drift from Middle-American tolerance to a witch's brew of hatreds. In April, Scott Hinckley gave his younger brother John his car, an old Camaro. John moved off campus to an apartment and signed up for the fall term at Texas Tech, where he stayed until dropping out the next spring. In April, 1976, John sold Scott's car to raise money for a trip to California. He flew west and did not write or call his parents for six weeks. On Mother's Day, John wrote home: "I hope this card finds you both well and in good spirits, despite your impossible younger son. I've taken a cozy, inexpensive apartment in Hollywood, Ca. I live about 3 blocks away from the famous Hollywood & Vine corner and two blocks away from the Sunset Strip. I was very lucky to find such a location because I am within easy walking distance of about 30 of the most famous music publishers in the world. I'm trying to sell some of my songs." A month later, Hinckley wrote his parents a dispirited letter: "Through a series of sorry circumstances, I am in trouble. For the past 2½ weeks I have literally been without food, shelter & clothing. On May 14, someone broke into my room and stole almost all of my possessions." He asked for money, which the Hinckleys sent, and, two weeks later, wrote about his discouraging search for work: "It's a miracle I still have my sanity after putting up with screaming kids and endless lines of Blacks, Mexicans, Chinese, and God knows what else." He also mentioned a contact at United Artists, who, he said, had encouraged him to form a duo, and asked if he should still look for work or stick with singing. In August, he wrote about a girlfriend, Lynn Collins, and mentioned cutting a "professional demo" at a studio ("I hope you're as optimistic about things to come as I am!"). In fact, John had had no success making contacts in the recording business, and Lynn Collins did not exist. During that summer, Hinckley saw *Taxi Driver* fifteen times at Hollywood's Egyptian Theater.

"The entire weird, phony, impersonal Hollywood scene" got to John in September, and he returned to Evergreen. His parents thought him "thin, agitated, and nervous." He worked as a busboy at a supper club, where he earned almost six hundred dollars through the early winter. "I was self-supporting for the first and only period in my life. I was 21 years old," he wrote in his autobiography. In March, he returned to Lubbock, where he remained through the summer of 1978. During that year, he complained of ailments —a sore eye, a sore throat, an earache, light-headedness— and he visited the Texas Tech clinic. He also became interested in the American Nazis—the National Socialist Party —in October, 1978, in Dallas. In the essay on his newfound antipathies, he claimed he "officially joined" the Nazi party, which he later denied. "By the summer of 1978," he wrote, "at the age of 23, I was an all-out anti-Semite and white racialist."

At the turn of the year, Hinckley moved back to Lubbock once more. In August, 1979, he bought a thirty-eight-caliber pistol at the Galaxy Pawn Shop, and in September, after he enrolled again at Texas Tech, he published a newsletter for the "American Front," which he called an "available alternative to the minority-kissing Republican and Democrat parties," "the Party for the proud White conservative who would rather wear coats and ties instead of swastikas and sheets." Calling himself National Director, Hinckley, now twenty-four, made up everything about the organization, including a list of members from thirty-seven states. Between January and November he moved three times, bringing to seventeen the number of places he had lived since leaving high school. At Christmas, Hinckley did not join his family. He told his parents he was going to New York to sell his novel, *It's a Mystery to Me;* instead he stayed in Lubbock. A picture of Hinckley taken in December shows him overweight, holding a gun to his temple.

In January, 1980, Hinckley had his first "anxiety attack," and had medical tests for dizziness. He also purchased a six-point-five-caliber rifle from Snidely Whiplash's Pawn Shop, for one hundred and five dollars. At the end of the month, he asked his parents if he could come home. "I was ailing in different areas," he later wrote John Hopper: "Perhaps it was psychosomatic; perhaps it wasn't." A doctor, who gave him a physical and diagnosed his throat problem as an allergy, prescribed Drixoral, an antihistamine. Hinckley weighed two hundred twenty-two pounds, sixty more than usual. He returned to Lubbock, where he formed a mail-order company called "Listalot," from which customers could buy lists of different types by responding to ads in magazines like *Country Style* and *The Nation.* The company was real, the lists imaginary. In May, *People* magazine reported that Jodie Foster was going to Yale, and the story planted the seed of the idea, which later took root, for Hinckley to travel to New Haven.

In June, he registered for the summer session at Texas

Tech, and he reported to the college clinic that he had been "on the firing range" and had trouble with his hearing. From the Empire Pawn Shop, he bought two boxes of bullets, including the exploding-head Devastators (he called them "stingers") he would use ten months later. His mother wrote him: "Hope your hearing is better today. I cannot believe you have so many crazy things happen to you." In late June, Hinckley went to a doctor, complaining of dizzy spells, palpitations, and fatigue. The doctor observed: "Patient showed a flat affect throughout examination and depressive reaction." He prescribed an antidepressant called Surmontil. To his sister Diane and her family, Hinckley wrote: "My nervous system is about shot. I take heavy medication for it which doesn't seem to do much good except make me very drowsy. By the end of the summer, I should be a bonafide basket case." After repeated visits to the doctor, Hinckley felt slightly better and asked for a mild tranquilizer. July 10: the doctor prescribed Valium for him to try. July 16: Hinckley purchased a twenty-two-caliber rifle from the Galaxy Pawn Shop. On July 17th, the doctor prescribed Valium for six weeks.

In August, Hinckley went to Colorado, to house-sit for his parents while they traveled in Europe, and he met with Darrell Benjamin, a psychologist who advised his father's company on personnel matters. Benjamin regarded Hinckley as a twenty-five-year-old who acted more like fourteen, and he recommended that Hinckley make a plan for his future. When Hinckley's parents returned in September, he signed an agreement with them: on the stock market, he could sell shares of Vanderbilt Energy stock, worth about thirty-six hundred dollars, to pay for a writing course at Yale University. He wrote: "Thank you for the money and one more chance." Hinckley left Denver for New Haven on September 17th, and on his arrival registered at the Sheraton Park Plaza, the city's major hotel. On the 19th, he wrote his sister and brother-in-law: "The students dress like total slobs. I'm going to NYC for the weekend. Classes at Yale are still up in the air. Is anything sacred anymore?" On the 20th, he spoke by phone with Jodie Foster and taped the conversation. He did the same on the 22nd, and then flew back to Colorado. He wrote in his autobiography: "My mind was on the breaking point. A relationship I had dreamed about went absolutely nowhere. My disillusionment with EVERYTHING was complete."

On the 26th, Hinckley flew to Lubbock and bought two twenty-two-caliber pistols at Snidely Whiplash's. He also bought three thousand dollars' worth of American Express traveler's checks, with the proceeds from the sale of his Vanderbilt stock. On the 27th, he flew to Washington, D.C., where he sent a postcard to Diane and her family in Texas: "Yale is such a disappointment. These past weeks have been strange times. I keep getting hit over the head by reality. It doesn't feel very good." On the 28th, Hinckley flew from Washington to Columbus, Ohio, and on the 30th, he took a bus to Dayton. On October 2nd, President Carter visited Dayton. Hinckley decided not to shoot him. He put his guns in a locker, shook Carter's hand at the convention center, and left for New Haven, where he stayed for three days, leaving several notes for Jodie Foster. On October 6th, Hinckley flew to Lincoln, Nebraska, for a meeting that never took place with a member of the National Socialist Party, and on the 7th he made his way by plane to Nashville, Tennessee, via Chicago and New York. President Carter came to Nashville on the 9th, but Hinckley again changed his mind about shooting the President and hurried to catch a flight to New York. Airport guards found three pistols—two twenty-twos and a thirty-eight—in Hinckley's suitcase, along with a pair of handcuffs and a box of Winchester cartridges. He was arrested, charged with a misdemeanor, and fined sixty-two dollars and fifty cents. He carried about two thousand dollars in traveler's checks, slightly more than half of what he had gathered a few weeks before in cash and checks.

After holding him for four or five hours, the Nashville police drove Hinckley back to the airport and he returned to New Haven without his guns, which the police kept. On the 11th, he flew to Dallas, where he stayed with his sister. He went to Rocky's Police Equipment and bought two twenty-two-caliber pistols and two boxes of shells, for ninety-eight dollars and eighty cents. On the 15th, he went back to New Haven once more; on the 17th, he went to Washington for a few days; and on the 19th, running out of money, he returned to Denver.

Three days later, he took an overdose of Surmontil, the antidepressant that had been prescribed for him. His mother explained: "When I came home, I found John very ill. He appeared rather groggy and frantic. I suppose—or maybe he told me and I don't remember—that he took too many pills." The next week, for the first time, he met with psychiatrist John Hopper, at his parents' insistence. On Election Day, November 4th, Hinckley told Hopper about Jodie Foster; "I have two obsessions in life now: writing, and the person we discussed Nov. 4," he wrote Hopper soon after, "I care about nothing else!" At the end of the month, John sent an anonymous letter to the F.B.I.: "There is a plot underway to abduct actress Jodie Foster from Yale University dorm in December or January. No ransom. She's being taken for romantic reasons. This is no joke! I don't wish to get further involved. Act as you wish." The F.B.I. notified the head of Jodie Foster's dorm, who warned her about the threat. On November 30th, the day before Jack Hinckley returned from a mission in Africa with the Christian charity called World Vision, Hinckley told his mother he was going to Texas. He flew to Washington, where he stayed for two weeks. He had himself photographed in front of Ford's Theatre, where Abraham Lincoln was assassinated, and, outside Blair House, where the Reagans were living while the President-elect was being briefed, Hinckley saw Reagan several times. On one occasion, Hinckley carried a gun.

On December 8th, John Lennon was shot. Hinckley took the train to New York, and, in "deep mourning," he joined the Lennon vigil in Central Park. On December 14th, he went to New Haven and again left notes for Jodie Foster. On the 16th, he flew home to Evergreen and resumed sessions with Dr. Hopper. He made his New Year's Eve tape, and spent days walking around Denver shopping centers. In mid-January, he called Jodie Foster's number in New Haven. He also practiced shooting at a rifle-and-pistol range near Evergreen and, the day after the Presidential inauguration, he bought, in Denver, a thirty-eight, like the gun Mark David Chapman had used to shoot John Lennon. Between weekly appointments with Dr. Hopper, Hinckley flew east and registered at the Park Plaza in New Haven, under the name John Hudson. In February, Hinckley returned to New Haven for the eighth time. He left valentines and poems for Jodie Foster and went to New York. For the first time, rather than thinking of them as untouchable idols, he found himself interested in sex with women. He searched out prostitutes and, he later claimed, had intercourse with four, three of them teenagers.

On Valentine's Day, at ten-fifty—the hour John Lennon had been shot, but in the morning rather than the evening—Hinckley took a cab to the Dakota, where Lennon had lived. He intended to shoot himself, he said, but couldn't. He left for Washington the next day, returned to Evergreen for a night, went back to New Haven as John Hudson, and, on February 27th, had his last appointment with Dr. Hopper. On March 1st, Hinckley left for New York, after stealing a Krugerrand from his parents' home and selling it for five hundred dollars. He went to New Haven, where he left notes for Jodie Foster: "Just wait. I'll rescue you very soon. Please cooperate" and "Goodbye! I love you six trillion times. Don't you maybe like me just a little bit? (You must admit I am different.) It would make all of this worthwhile." On March 5th, he ran out of money, and early the next morning he called his parents; his father arranged for him to fly home. Jack Hinckley met his son at the airport, gave him two hundred and ten dollars, and sent him off on his own. John spent a night at Motel 6 in Denver and two weeks at the nearby Golden Hours Motel. To raise more money, he also sold a twenty-two- and a thirty-eight-caliber pistol and a six-point-five-caliber rifle to Larry of Lakewood, an independent dealer who had advertised in the paper, and sold his guitar and typewriter to G.I. Joe's Pawn Shop for fifty dollars. On March 23rd, after the police tracked down Hinckley at the Golden Hours Motel because he looked suspicious, he moved back to Motel 6 and registered as J. Travis. Two days later, his mother drove him to the airport. Hinckley spent a day in Hollywood and on March 26th, after switching buses in Los Angeles, he took a Greyhound through Cleveland and Pittsburgh to Washington. He arrived on March 29th, in the early afternoon, and went to the Park Central Hotel.

On the 30th, after a poor night's sleep, he got up, took a Valium, and went out for breakfast at McDonald's. He came back to his room and tried to doze. On the way back from breakfast, he had picked up the *Washington Star* and, when he couldn't sleep, he opened the paper and noticed the President's schedule, on page A-4. It was almost noon.

Hinckley took a shower, and, when his mind started to run, he took more Valium to calm down. He loaded his twenty-two with Devastator bullets, and wrote the letter to Jodie Foster that he left in his hotel room. At about one-thirty, wearing a jacket because of the drizzle, with a red John Lennon button in his left pocket and his gun in the right, he took a cab to the Washington Hilton, where the President was scheduled to speak to a labor convention at quarter to two. The President waved as he went into the hotel, and Hinckley waved back. Time seemed to him to speed up. When the President came out at two-twenty-five, Hinckley waited until he could step within firing range, and he emptied the cylinder of his gun.

In Hinckley's wallet after the shooting, the police found a card on which was printed the Second Amendment of the United States Constitution ("A well regulated Militia, being necessary to the security of a free State, the right of the people to keep and bear arms shall not be infringed"), a Colorado identity card, a Texas driver's license, one hundred and twenty-nine dollars in cash, a photo of his nephew Chris, and several pictures of Jodie Foster. In one, she was heavily made up as *Esquire*'s vision of a coed, biting her lower lip and holding a basketball. In another, she looked years younger than her true age, like a model for a junior-high-school yearbook picture. In room 312 of the Park Central Hotel, where Hinckley had stayed, police found two small suitcases; an empty box of Devastator bullets and another box of bullets; an Army fatigue jacket and a number of wool lumberjack shirts; an article about the writer Frances FitzGerald from *Esquire*; a 1981 Lennon Color Calendar; a Band-Aid box with a folded note at its bottom ("This plane has been hijacked! I have a bomb with me. Plus flammable liquids and a knife. A companion is also on the plane with a firearm. Act naturally and lead the way to the cabin. Stay calm!"); a postcard with a picture of President and Mrs. Reagan on one side and a note to Jodie Foster on the other ("Don't they make a darling couple? Nancy is downright sexy. One day you and I will occupy the White House and the peasants will drool with envy. Until then, please do your best to remain a virgin. You are a virgin, aren't you?"); several paperback books (including *The Fan,* by Bob Randall; *The Catcher in the Rye,* by J. D. Salinger; *The Skyjacker,* by David G. Hubbard; *The Fox is Crazy Too,* by Eliot Asinof; *Romeo and Juliet;* and *Taxi Driver*); a picture of Napoleon and Josephine labeled "John and Jodie"; an array of pills, from nonprescription standards like Tylenol, to Drixoral, Surmontil, and Valium; and thirty-eight pages of Hinckley's own writings.

From 1973 on, John Hinckley had no friends and few acquaintances. He could count on seeing his brother only at Christmas, and his sister and her family more often, on visits to Dallas and at Christmas. Hinckley maintained contact with his parents, speaking or corresponding with them irregularly, but he didn't tell them his deepest concerns. They never knew about Jodie Foster or *Taxi Driver,* and they did not know about his travels across the country; they did not know about his arrest in Nashville, and they thought he was in Texas when he was stalking the President. Hinckley kept most of these facts from his psychiatrist, Dr. Hopper, as well. Hinckley's main forms of expression were music and writing, and dozens of his poems, short stories, essays, letters, postcards, and other scribblings were entered into evidence at his trial. They depicted a bleak, restless life, and gave the trial's tumble of evidence a peculiar coherence, while fixing on paper its creepy, oppressive feel.

Hinckley's short stories delivered obvious messages. An attempt at a fairy tale, called "Katy by the Numbers," about a land of Countless Numbers, ends abruptly when Katy realizes that the numbers exist without trees or houses or anything else resembling a normal world. "Dream In Disgrace," about a weary chess player who loses a tournament match to a boy, ends: "Nathan sighed, then stumbled into the bathroom, removed a straightedge razor from the cabinet, and put his dream out of its misery." "Son of a Gun Collector," Hinckley's favorite of his stories, tracks a showdown between father and son. Against orders, the son touches his father's prized gun; the father disciplines his son; the son touches the gun again; the father rages; the son shoots his father and says, "Don't worry, Mama . . . From now on, I'll be the man in the house."

In a treatment for a film called *West of Denver*, Hinckley all but parodies himself. He presents the "story of a boy 18, just out of high school, disturbed, living in the past, the Wild West. His life is the Old West. He hates the modern day world. He lives in a small western-type town west of Denver. (Evergreen)." The main character is Jamie: "Jamie is a loner with many psychological problems. He is without a summer job and has time on his hands." Jamie loads a gun and shoots from a hill at cars and trucks on a highway. The treatment closes with lines for the sheriff's deputies: "What a strange kid he is!" "That boy needs psychiatric attention and fast." For a college theme about a personal belief, Hinckley chose "People Are Violent, Cruel and Selfish." His teacher commented, "A personal belief should involve you more than this seems to. What have you omitted?"

After John Lennon's death, John Hinckley wrote a bitter essay, which he called, "I read the news today, oh no!" after a line from a Beatles song: "John Lennon is dead and people continue to laugh and dream and live. I'll be damned if I understand it. Oh, listen to the comedian tell his jokes about airplanes and telephone operators. Isn't he funny, just hysterical. The audience is laughing so he must be amusing. But I'm not too close to a smile. John Lennon is dead!" The heart of the essay could be read as a brief for gun control: "In America, heroes are meant to be killed. Idols are meant to be shot in the back. Guns are neat little things, aren't they? They can kill extraordinary people with very little effort. But don't say a word about it to the NRA." The piece repeats its theme ("John Lennon died a couple of weeks ago and I died too. Bang, bang, we're all dead") and ends: "The dream died. I died. You died. Everyone died. America died. The world died. The universe died," trailing off in illegible musings about God.

Hinckley's poems, scores of them, prompted the most comment from witnesses at trial. Their titles are like names on a punk-rock record album: "Guns are Fun!," "42nd Street Love," "Give Me," "Burning Out." The first one alone could quench all thirst for interpretation. To the outraged, it reads like a boast:

> See that living legend over there?
> With one little squeeze of this trigger
> I can put that person at my feet
> moaning and groaning and pleading with God.

As with other Hinckley writings, the tone might be considered sardonic:

> This gun gives me pornographic power.
> If I wish, the president will fall
> and the world will look at me in disbelief,
>
> all because I own an inexpensive gun.
> Guns are lovable, Guns are fun
> Are you lucky enough to own one?

The poems in which Hinckley's voice reaches for notes of anguish and revelation have titles like "Prince Valium," "The Elephant Man and I," and "The Painful Evolution." From "Prince Valium":

You know a few things about me, dear sweetheart
Like my obsession with fantasy
But what the rabble don't yet understand
Is that fantasies become reality in my world.

From "The Elephant Man and I":

Perhaps the Elephant Man would understand my dilemma
We seem to have so many precious things in common
It's all a question of face to face communication.

"The Painful Evolution" reads:

In the beginning
it was a time for pretending.
The martyr in me played games
and I was the young alienated loner.

Toward the middle,
I lied about pain and troubles.
It was a mere three years ago
that I played the part so well.

Nearing the bend,
I should have turned back.
I could have taken the road
that leads to a meaningful existence.

In the end,
I cursed myself and suffered.
I have become what I wanted
to be all along, a psychotic poet.

In the poem "Regardless," he writes, "I continue to grovel for normalcy," and, in "Midnight Prayers," "nothing seems to soothe my rage." Hinckley's only poems of hope, how-ever tentative, deal with Jodie Foster, as in "I know a Girl":

> I know a girl who is beyond words;
> I don't know her well but I know her.
> I know she knows that I know her
> and she knows that I love her.
> I don't know her true feelings towards me
> but she knows that I know her name.

In Hinckley's world, the poet breathes no joy and never sighs with relief. He buries fundamental questions in throw-away lines:

> Can you reach over and turn off
> the television set so we can talk?

CHAPTER FOUR

The
Adams
Trial

A FEW WEEKS before the Hinckley trial got under way in Washington, a local case provided a sample of an insanity defense, and a control for the more celebrated event. Of the insanity cases that go to trial each year in the District of Columbia, almost all occur in local court. Even with its own case law and rules of procedure, like the fifty states, the District has unique status because the federal government plays a direct role in the administration of D.C. justice. In 1970, Congress passed a special act, which, for the District only, set out a law of insanity based on the ALI model. The statute also provided for Presidential appointment of local judges and for the United States Attorney and his staff, who prosecute federal cases, to handle local matters. The Public Defender Service, which the law established to assure adequate counsel for the poor, does most of the defense work.

The Brawner opinion revealed "our well-guarded secret that the great majority of responsibility cases concern indigents, not affluent defendants with easy access to legal and psychiatric assistance." Insanity defendants in Washington tend to be poor, young, black men—like Rufus Adams, who was on trial for six counts of murder, rape, and sodomy of a young black woman. In February, 1982, in the first stage of a two-part trial, a jury had found Adams guilty of committing all the acts with which he was charged. In April, the same jury was brought back to consider Adams's insanity plea. The so-called bifurcated trial, which was designed in 1925 by a California crime commission to protect the state from surprise insanity defenses, separates the question "Did he do it?" from "Was he responsible?" It also lets the defendant use an unusual logic. "I didn't do it," he can argue, "but if the jury thinks I did, then I was insane." Along with the District, five states have permitted the procedure—although a couple of them later rescinded it, and others have ruled that evidence about the defendant's intent must be admissible at both stages of a trial, defeating the invention's purpose of limiting psychiatric testimony to a secondary forum. In the District, the defendant can choose between a regular and a two-step trial.

The Adams jury was composed of eleven blacks and one white, seven women and five men—the same breakdown as the Hinckley jury. In 1982, Washington's population was seventy percent black, and the District's jury pool was drawn from lists of voters and drivers. After excusing policemen, firemen, members of the armed services, public officials, nurses, clergymen, teachers, doctors, lawyers, and others, the federal and local courts were left with veniremen, the people who were called and showed up for duty. In a session called *voir dire*—from the French, to speak the truth—counsel for both sides could challenge potential jurors on grounds that they knew the defendant, had predetermined convictions about the case, or otherwise showed prejudice. The first dozen unchallenged veniremen made up a jury, with alternates filling out a panel in case a regular member dropped off. A jury of working-class blacks is not unusual in the District. In a 1982 sampling of 9409 jurors qualified for duty in federal or local court that was reported by law to the Administrative Office of the United States Courts, fifty-four percent were women and forty-six percent men, seventy-eight percent were non-white and twenty-two percent white.

In the Adams case, Chief Judge Carl Moultrie, of the local trial court, presided over experienced counsel—for the prosecution, Steven Gordon, the head of the felony trial division of the United States Attorney's office; for the defense, Gary Kohlman, director of the Public Defender Service trial section, and an assistant, William Traylor. To explain why Rufus Adams had attacked Alfreda Garner, a prostitute whom he had known for less than a week, Kohlman offered a theory that sounded like a Freudian cartoon. Adams was born in Washington in 1945, the son of a stern father and a protective mother, and had, said Kohlman, "at a very early age . . . exhibited signs of . . . sexual confusion." By his teens he had snatched a number of pocketbooks, and by his late teens he had committed several sexual assaults. Adams spent the first years of his twenties in a correctional center, where doctors noted in him paranoia and confused sexual tendencies. He was on the street for a couple of years and then spent seven years in prison after convictions for three more sexual assaults. In 1978 he was paroled, and within a year of his release his parents died and his job at a prison dairy ended. He moved in with an old friend. Nine years earlier, Adams and his roommate had carried on a homosexual affair; in an odd twist when they lived together again, Adams's friend wore women's clothing and was preparing for a sex-change operation.

Adams eventually moved out, and for the first time in his life he lived alone, in a boardinghouse where he thought the smoke detector was a listening device.

Prosecutor Gordon offered a cartoon of his own, in the spirit of Darwin rather than Freud: Rufus Adams had pursued a life of crime from the age of nineteen. He planned each crime carefully, and each time he went to St. Elizabeths for evaluation, the government hospital found no mental diseases or defects. Doctors found Adams manipulative and dangerous, but not ill. When he killed Alfreda Garner with a knife and garrote in a brutal crime, the prosecution contended, Adams knew right from wrong and could conform his conduct to the requirements of the law. He was a conniver, and a survivor.

During the week occupied by Adams's trial, the respective styles of the judge, lawyers, and witnesses eclipsed what they said about the defendant, and the defendant never said a word. In contrast to Judge Parker in the Hinckley case, whose quest for fairness made him edgy, Judge Moultrie soothed the courtroom. Earnest and determined, prosecutor Steven Gordon wore wing-tip shoes with thick soles, and he stroked his neat moustache methodically between comments. William Traylor, for the defense, was a fine-boned black man, with a small bald spot and close-cropped hair, and he looked unnervingly like the defendant. Most compelling of all, defense lawyer Gary Kohlman defied convention. His thick brown hair ended abruptly at his shoulders, and under counsel's table he tucked a wide-brim cowboy hat. His beard was trimmed like a woodsman's and he used his hands and voice with restraint, punctuating his speeches for Adams with small gestures.

Once the trial got rolling, one of the defendant's two brothers testified that, when he was twelve or thirteen, "I was approached by my brother. My father and mother were not home at the time; just he and myself were there. He had approached me sexually." In a deep, sarcastic voice, the prosecutor asked him, "Do you conclude, sir, that just because your brother once made a homosexual pass at you, that he was *insane?*" Another brother said Rufus hadn't talked with anyone in the family when he was released from prison, and had accused them of "a whole lot of things." He asserted, "I would say he was mentally disturbed." The prosecutor scowled, then pressed, in an exchange that boiled down to one implicit point.

"You were raised in the same household with Mr. Rufus Adams, Jr.; is that correct?"

"Yes."

"Have you ever received mental treatment?"

"I have never received mental treatment."

"And in your opinion, sir, are you in need of mental treatment?"

"No."

The prosecutor's last, unspoken, question flowed naturally from the others:

"If you're all right, isn't Rufus?"

Tonya Johnson, who was Tony when she first met Rufus Adams, was tall and big-boned, with shoulder-length corn-rows. She spoke with a slight lisp and eyed the ceiling vacantly when she was not sure how to answer a question. She said Adams "was a little bit too perfect . . . because of him being incarcerated for such a long time." The Reverend Cecil J. Cheeks, huge and black, wearing a shirt marked "Peoples Drugs," claimed he had known Adams since 1975 and that since 1976 Adams had been "very, very paranoid. . . . [He] constantly watched things that was going on around him." On direct examination, Cheeks led the court to believe that he had met Adams in a prison counseling program, in his capacity as a minister working with men behind bars. On cross-examination, the prosecutor asked Cheeks if he and Adams had met when both men were serving time in prison, and if vigilance—to "watch their backs"—weren't a useful trait for prisoners. "Correct, sir," Cheeks agreed to both questions, and the prosecutor advised, after a run of other questions designed to impeach the witness, "I have nothing further, Your Honor."

Expert testimony lasted five days. The jury listened stoically and the gallery dwindled to a hard core of three or four. Appearing for the defense, Dr. Dorothy Evans diagnosed Adams as a paranoid schizophrenic who had trouble looking at the world in realistic terms, and trouble with his feelings about sex and aggression. She was slim, attractive, and black, a doctor of clinical psychology, and she told the jury she divided her time between psychotherapy, teaching, and community mental-health work. Her inexperience as a witness paid off for the defense. She described her interviews with Adams clearly and with none of the condescension that frequent witnesses pick up through years of talking to jurors who can't talk back. As the defendant sat quietly a few strides from the witness stand, raising his eyebrows and stroking his chin, Evans answered questions put by both sides. Did Adams look crazy? No, he protected himself by appearing orderly. Why did he kill Alfreda Garner? He thought women had the capacity to take care of him, if only they would; he idolized them, and hated them, and, if they didn't help him, he would hurt them.

The prosecution's expert, Dr. A. David Shapiro, found no mental disorder in Adams. In his view, the defendant showed "an excellent range of emotion" and "no consistent or pervasive evidence of any mental disorder on the tests," although "he does have some difficulty with controlling his own feelings." Shapiro was a forensic psychologist, trained for courtroom work, and he had been on the staff of St.

Elizabeths before setting up a private practice. Small, white, and balding, with thick glasses and a nose-wrinkling sniffle that was amplified by a microphone on the witness stand, he admitted that Adams did not give normal responses to questions, but insisted the defendant was sane.

A long diary, which Rufus Adams had kept until ten days after the crime, was the trial's Rosetta stone. "Vibes say smoke alarm is really a listening device," he scratched. "I check it out." "Vibes say they want to pick up the tapes." "FBI, CIA were there." "The whole area was loaded with dirty clothes cops." Kohlman concluded, "The man has fallen completely apart. . . . Does that make him a victim? . . . Of course it doesn't." But the defense lawyer suggested that Adams was sick and needed help. Gordon asked the only question that mattered. "[I]s that the crime of someone who does not know what he is doing and who is out of control, or is that the crime of someone who has an evil, twisted, perverted mind?" He answered, "Rufus Adams is sick, ladies and gentlemen, but he's not crazy."

The judge closed the trial by reading instructions of law, of which two were key: the jury had to rule separately on each count; if they found the defendant not guilty by reason of insanity on any count, he would go to St. Elizabeths for fifty days' evaluation of his current mental status. The judge also instructed that, on the question of insanity, the defense had the burden of proof, by a preponderance of the evidence. After three days, the jurors returned a verdict. On the first five counts, they found Adams guilty. On the sixth —sodomy committed after he killed Alfreda Garner, who was known as Rita—the jury found him not guilty by reason of insanity. The result fit statistics from the Public Defender Service from 1979 through 1983: of the 525 jury trials the Service handled in that period, none resulted in an undivided verdict of not guilty by reason of insanity. The

Service's twenty-six insanity acquittals came in trials before judges only, and all but two were uncontested.

With his head down, eyes closed, and one hand caressing his forehead, Rufus Adams listened to the judge poll the members of the jury. He shook hands with his lawyers, and followed a marshal through a back door of the courtroom to pick up his belongings at the city jail and go to St. Elizabeths. Half of the jurors stayed around to explain their verdict. "I felt like he was sick but knew what he was doing." "The man definitely needs some help." "That's not a normal thing, for a man to sodomize a dead body." "We really came to the conclusion that he was somewhat insane. We realized he needed help, even though he was aware of what he was doing." "We were sending a message to the court. We think Mr. Adams needs treatment, but we didn't want him furloughed after fifty days, because he would be a menace to the community." "I feel the man needed help, but I would never want to see him on the street, at least for a long time." "I'll tell you one thing: this case does a terrific job of indicting the system. He had two counts of armed rape, but, way back when, there were indications that he was a paranoid schizophrenic, and no one did anything about it? Whose fault is that?"

In the basement of the Public Defender Service, near the District of Columbia courthouse, the office of Gary Kohlman held the records of a decade of trial work. Piles of transcripts and legal briefs filled a shopping cart in front of the door, a stuffed couch against the wall, and most of the top of a large wooden desk. They also covered the floor, like abandoned stumps in the waste of a forest. In front of a window, a rubber plant sat in a large pail, and behind the desk, on a sill or on the wall, were unbalanced scales of justice, a drawing of a P-38 fighter plane, and a wilderness calendar with a picture of a kayaker in white water. Kohlman was as unceremonious as the office. Before the verdict came in, he put his feet on the desk and talked about the insanity defense.

"I think it's a good idea," he began. "The community has a strong sense of the difference between cases where defendants are just dangerous and where defendants present mitigating circumstances, like mental illness, and should be acquitted. My job is to help the jury understand how the defendant is vulnerable. The jury usually wants to help, if the verdict won't jeopardize the community, so I have to humanize the defendant. The amount of money I have to spend on a case doesn't really affect the outcome: I'll spend three or four thousand dollars on the Adams case, which is a lot for this office, but the facts in the case will be more important to the jury than the money. No matter how many experts I parachute into trial, I have to give the jury a reason to find Mr. Adams not guilty, and convince the jurors that they can do it without hurting the community. I know for sure I'd rather have him in St. Elizabeths than prison, and that's what I work for."

On the way over to court to hear the verdict, Kohlman took a piece of paper out of his pocket. He said, "This rounds out the issues some," and offered an unsigned letter:

Dear Mr. Kohlman:

Your defense of Rufus Adams makes you an accessory to his crimes, the one he is accused of committing and those he has committed that we don't know about. You are as guilty as he.

Perhaps one day a member of your family will be assaulted, raped or even murdered by someone like Mr. Adams whose attorney was talented enough to get him off a criminal charge. You also, because of your actions, will bear the guilt of that crime.

One of the real shames of our system is that we don't have laws to deal with people like you. Unfortunately, though, that is how our system works. It is impossible to write laws that appeal to a person's sense of morality, and it is beyond me to imagine how you, obviously a talented lawyer, can be so lacking in moral judgment.

It may be because of your idealistic attitudes, why else could you work so hard to let a man like Rufus Adams out on the street again? But where will your idealistic attitudes be in three years when you are working in a posh law firm, living in the suburbs, driving a Porsche while other people who live in this city have to deal with Mr. Adams after his "mental problems have been solved."

I have probably given you more time than you deserve.

CHAPTER FIVE

Money

THE COMPUTER printout listing all the legal papers filed in the Hinckley case during the year before trial stretched to fifteen feet, like the index for a prolonged antitrust case, but the hours spent by lawyers in preparing them hardly represented the full cost of the case. Doctors spent hundreds of hours interviewing Hinckley to ascertain his state of mind at the moment of the shooting. One court-appointed psychiatrist, who eventually took the stand for the government, spent over fifty-seven hours with Hinckley; in most cases, a few hours is the maximum. The doctors for the government charged over three hundred thousand dollars in fees and expenses, and those for the defense about half that. Security for the trial cost over a million dollars.

The defense team consisted of a senior partner, a junior partner, and two associates of an expensive Washington firm, Williams & Connolly, which has earned a first-rate reputation as counsel for white-collar criminal defendants —clients accused of corruption, corporations charged with securities violations, and the like. Had these lawyers billed only half the time they spent working on the case during the year and a quarter between its start and finish, which sometimes happens for extraordinary clients, standard charges would have easily topped half a million dollars.

The government's costs were probably even higher. For a year and a quarter, the government assigned three lawyers, two F.B.I. agents, one Secret Service agent, and three metropolitan police officers to the case full time, with others to back them up, and used dozens of F.B.I., Secret Service, and other officers to chase down facts. Their most expensive hunt ended up with almost no yield for the trial. While he was in solitary confinement at the federal penitentiary in Butner, North Carolina, during the months before trial, John Hinckley scribbled an account of the shooting that included a bombshell. "There were 8 other people involved in the plots to kill President Carter and President Reagan," he avowed; "I was anything but a lone gunman on March 30, 1981."

Hinckley's scheme began, he wrote, when he placed a classified ad in *Soldier of Fortune* magazine in July, 1979 ("TO ALL CONSERVATIVES—are you fed up with the cowardly, ineffective Republican party? Write N.F.P., 2404 10th Street #208, Lubbock, TX 79401"). His chronicle gave the last name of one co-conspirator ("Tropmann") and initials for others. He promised, "I have the power to implicate 8 other dangerous people, 2 of them quite well known." The story would be a bargaining chip. He "wanted to help," but only if the government made "extraordinary concessions."

The government seized the sheets on which Hinckley recorded this story after the words "prison," "life sentence," and "cooperation with the Justice Department" caught the eye of a guard at the correctional institution. The F.B.I. promptly scurried around the country to investigate the claims; scores of agents worked for weeks on the assignment. The government postponed Hinckley's arraignment in court until the Bureau finished the inquiry. Finding no reliable evidence to corroborate Hinckley's tale of conspiracy, the F.B.I. concluded that the deed was his alone—but not until the costs of handling Hinckley's case had mounted even higher.

All of these expenses did not include the costs of doctors on federal salaries, who did not submit bills for the time they spent on the case, or the cost of the judge and his law clerks, who were already on the federal payroll. Medical, security, and legal costs alone reached two and a half to three million dollars. The Hinckley case also fueled the media (thirty to forty reporters covered the trial each day for two months, including a half-dozen sketch artists and a dozen broadcast reporters who were backed up by quartets of sound and camera crews), filled the gallery (daily attendance of reporters and visitors averaged around one hundred; over two thousand people signed the court's daily visitor's book, after waiting in line up to three hours, and some came to almost every session), and spawned a cottage industry for transcripts (the court reporter charged fifty cents a page for each of the ten thousand pages of pre-trial and trial transcripts, and twenty-five cents a page if a collector bought all the pages for a half-day session, which usually ran to 125 pages; the lawyers in the case shared a bill from the court reporter for seventy thousand dollars). Jurors were paid thirty dollars a day during the first month of the trial and thirty-five dollars during the second.

The government's doctors charged more overall than the defense's, and the federal costs of the trial were at least three times the costs for the Hinckleys, but the family's wealth enhanced the trial's immoderate character. Jack Hinckley called Vanderbilt Energy Corporation a "very small publicly owned oil-and-gas-exploration company," and, in the scale of that industry, he was correct. But the company was prosperous enough to support a score of employees and to permit Jack Hinckley to devote a portion of his time to volunteer work around the world, with World Vision, a Christian charity. In a dozen years, Vanderbilt had grown from nothing to dominion over resources from the Texas Gulf to the Rocky Mountains. The family's prosperity allowed them to hire Williams & Connolly, whose aggressive advocacy, along with that of the prosecution, helped make the trial a vigorous contest.

CHAPTER SIX

Psychiatry
and the
Law

NEXT TO THE CENTRAL tug-of-war about John Hinck-ley's sanity, the pull between the disciplines of psychiatry and the law was the strongest of several tensions in the trial. Had the doctors in the case been treating the defendant, they presumably would have worked out differences of opinion over his diagnosis through consultation. Differences of opinion would have been significant only if they had led to varying conclusions about what treatment to prescribe. In court, however, the stark choice between a conviction and a finding of not guilty by reason of insanity pushed the doctors and their differing opinions to opposite poles and identified them with one option versus the other. The courtroom dispute also gave a distorted picture of psychiatry, since it is generally-accepted wisdom that doctors agree on psychiatric diagnoses in about eighty percent of cases. The challenge of diagnosing Hinckley at an instant in history and using that conclusion as a basis for judging his criminal responsibility was essentially a legal one. Doctors who regularly take on such challenges are called forensic psychiatrists, and they often have reputations as hired guns, no matter how good they are as psychiatrists. Of thirty thousand American psychiatrists, less than a thousand are forensic psychiatrists, and only a hundred and twenty-five of these regularly testify on criminal responsibility. These and other psychiatrists recognize that it is a difficult enough task to treat someone in the present, without the added problem of trying to diagnose his past behavior, based on evidence that is often prejudiced and stale.

In court, the doctors preferred to speak about mental disorder; the lawyers, using the terms of the insanity defense, referred to mental disease or defect. Whatever John Hinckley's mental illness was called, it did not guarantee that he would be found legally insane. The insanity law in the District of Columbia required, first, that psychiatrists find he suffered from a mental abnormality, and, second, that the jury find he could not—as a result of the abnormality—tell right from wrong or abide by the law. The glossary for the doctors' debate was the *Diagnostic and Statistical Manual of Mental Disorders (Third Edition)*, known informally as DSM-III.

The American Psychiatric Association published the volume's first edition in 1952. As an introduction to the third edition explains, the first and second did not provide "explicit criteria" for mental disorders; doctors were on their own to define the "contents and boundaries of the diagnostic categories" from clinical experience. After heated debate within the A.P.A., the third edition "provides specific diagnostic criteria as guides for making each diagnosis," and, in field tests, doctors have applied these criteria with eighty to ninety percent agreement for severe mental illnesses and sixty to seventy percent agreement for less severe disorders. The criteria lead some lawyers and doctors to call DSM-III a cookbook, and the introduction to the latest manual offers several disclaimers: "In DSM-III there is no assumption that each mental disorder is a discrete entity with sharp boundaries (discontinuity) between it and other mental disorders, as well as between it and No Mental Disorder. . . ." "A common misconception is that a classification of mental disorders classifies individuals, when actually what are being classified are disorders that individuals have. For this reason, the text of DSM-III avoids the use of such phrases as 'schizophrenic' or 'an alcoholic,' and instead uses the more accurate, but admittedly more wordy 'an individual with Alcohol Dependence.' " One doctor, in an attempt to find a legal analogy, called the DSM-III the statute law of psychiatry. Given the debate within the psychiatric profession about the book and its evolution, he might have called it a statement of psychiatry's common law, to be applied and supplemented according to the experience, training, and idiosyncracies of each judge.

John Hopper was the first doctor to take the stand. Angular and tanned, he wore aviator glasses and blinked slowly before answering the questions of lawyers from both sides. He spoke in a weary voice, as if, for him, the trial was a bad dream he hoped to put to rest by explaining why he handled John Hinckley as he did, from October, 1980, through February, 1981. From the start, the defense lawyers suggested, he had discounted signs of the seriousness of Hinckley's illness. When the Hinckleys told Hopper of John's suicide attempt, the doctor didn't ask to see him right away. Instead, Hopper telephoned John to ask if he had really tried to kill himself. Hopper's notes on the four months of treatment consisted of fourteen pages, a few of them with only two or three lines of comments. Three of them dealt with the "severe marital discord" of Jack and JoAnn Hinckley. When the notes listed "what's been tried," the entries were from the parents' perspective: "Being patient, abiding him, doctors, giving money." In Hopper's view, John was a "typical case" in Evergreen, frustrated by his inability to "get anywhere in writing" or to keep up with the rest of a successful family. According to Hopper, a plan ("setting some goals and objectives") and biofeedback ("the use of equipment which shows a person either visually or auditorially in which direction relaxation is going") were the proper treatment for Hinckley's depression and anxiety. After twenty-two sessions with John Hinckley, at sixty dollars an hour, the doctor knew nothing of John's trips to Hollywood, his extreme interest in *Taxi Driver,* his fantastic reading, his failure to enroll in any program at Yale when he went to New Haven to meet Jodie Foster, his trip to Dayton, his arrest in Nashville, his target practice, his travels around the country, or his plan to kill the President. Because of Hopper's role as the defendant's one-time therapist, John Hinckley's lawyers could not afford to ridicule the doctor. But they presented him as a witness of fact and not as a medical expert. They tried to use the doctor's failure to recognize John's symptoms as evidence of a wily illness: Hinckley had fooled even a trained psychiatrist.

At the end of his testimony, Hopper asked to talk with the judge. Judge Parker called the lawyers to the bench. "I don't have the slightest idea what this man is going to say and I don't want to hear him," the judge reported. A lawyer for the defense surmised, "I think he may be concerned because there is the impression in the jury's mind right now that he did not believe that John Hinckley was suffering from a mental illness. . . . There is something still bothering the man." The judge responded, "Well, there is something that bothers everybody in this case." While court was in session, the judge would not hear another word out of Hopper.

The lead expert for the defense was William Carpenter, a psychiatrist who studied and treated schizophrenia, from the University of Maryland. He was a tall man with a silvery beard and shoulder-length hair, and folded into the witness stand, he resembled Father Time. He spoke in a smoky drawl, and his meandering answers tested the patience of the judge. "I need to keep the dates straight to look at it here because there are so many different places he has gone over the next few days," said Carpenter, referring to Hinckley's travels in the month before the shooting. "But he left Denver on February the 9th, flew to New York and went to New Haven. On the 16th he comes back to Washington. On the 18th he goes back to New Haven. On the 19th he goes back to Denver—he is going to New Haven to leave materials to make contact with Jodie Foster. At this point, he is having to deal with intense impulses around Jodie Foster and around terminating his own life. He feels that he is on a roller coaster, and cannot escape. He has developed, in some sense, multiple plans for how he might remove himself from this. The plans that are most intense on his mind involve killing himself in front of Jodie Foster, shooting Jodie Foster, then killing himself, shooting to wound her and then killing himself, killing her and then killing himself. At times, he has plans, thoughts, or impulses about going to a classroom, shooting the professor, the various students, and then killing himself—the classroom that Jodie Foster would be in. He also spent some time during the trips looking for a young prostitute that he had seen and he thinks is about twelve years old—again, this character Iris that Jodie Foster played in the movie—spending time searching for her, looking for her. His trip to Washington —he came to Washington, he doesn't have a strong sense of what he is doing, of why he is doing that. He has a strong sense of why he is going to New Haven and Yale. He spends time in the city, goes to the Capitol, goes to Senator Tower's office, goes to Senator Kennedy's office. There are some notions about—but these pass very quickly—about whether he would try to assassinate Senator Kennedy. His attention is brought to materials he has read about the Puerto Rican nationalist shooting in the House of Representatives some years ago. He gets on his mind the possibility of getting into the galleries and shooting a number of Representatives, pictures himself with his weaponry, with his arms in the gallery and how much shooting he could do before he was shot. His state of mind during the time is depression, the need to terminate all of this, to have his own death. Of the impulses to be destructive to others, the most persistent is the destruction of Jodie Foster."

Dr. Carpenter diagnosed John Hinckley as suffering from a major depressive disorder and from process schizophrenia, a form of illness that begins in adolescence or early adulthood and progresses to a severe disorder marked by breaks from reality, magical thinking, and ideas of reference strong enough to be delusions—the belief that normal events, like President Reagan waving at a crowd or Jodie Foster appearing on television, were happening just for Hinckley. Calm, sympathetic, yet clinical, Carpenter described a condition and acts for which, he said, Hinckley could not be held responsible.

Park Dietz, a forensic psychiatrist, led the government's expert witnesses, and its team of doctors. At about $120,000, his fees and expenses topped those of the other doctors. In a high, prim voice, he spoke the lingo of his profession, the medical version of cop-talk. Large and carefully groomed, he had full cheeks and a quizzical brow. For whatever reason, sketch artists at the trial stumbled over Dietz, and said they made him look evil when they didn't mean to. Dietz was thirty-three years old. Although he testified for five days, he was not long-winded. His precision surprised even the prosecutor. At one session, Dietz dispatched a dull question with a vivid response. "Is that your metaphor?" the prosecutor asked, to extend the impact of the answer. "I believe it's a simile," Dietz corrected, with a faint smile.

He was full of numbers: interviews of the government doctors with John Hinckley, interviews with witnesses to the crime, visits with Hinckley's family, hours spent analyzing facts, the length of the government's report on Hinckley's sanity. The report cropped up repeatedly, although it was never admitted in evidence. The prosecutors and Dietz reminded the court that it was 628 pages long, with a 180-page summary. In a section of the report called "Psychiatric Assessment," the government's psychiatric team diagnosed John Hinckley as suffering from dysthymic disorder, or depressive neurosis, and from three types of personality disorder—schizoid, narcissistic, and mixed—the last with borderline and passive-aggressive features. This diagnosis was less grave than that of the defense's doctors; to some, "but not the government's," "borderline" implied an illness approaching psychosis. "The defendant's dysthymic disorder is relatively persistent," the report stated, "and there is no evidence of periods of normal mood lasting more than a month." Hinckley suffered "marked loss of interest or pleasure in most of his activities, sleep disturbance, feelings of chronic tiredness, perceptions of low self-esteem and self-depreciation, decreased ability to attend and concentrate, loss of interest in or enjoyment of pleasurable activities, recurrent thoughts of death or suicide, and a pessimistic attitude towards the future."

As evidence of Hinckley's alleged schizoid personality disorder, the team found "emotional coldness and aloofness and an absence of warm or tender feelings for others; indifference to praise or criticism or to the feelings of others; an absence of close relationships."

His narcissistic personality disorder was manifest, they said, in "a grandiose sense of self-importance or uniqueness (with exaggerations of achievements and talents); preoccupation with fantasies of unlimited success and ideal love; the search for constant attention."

They also found "feelings of cool indifference and marked feelings of inferiority, shame, and emptiness in response to perceptions of defeat and failure; and the presence in interpersonal relationships of feelings of entitlement, alternating between extremes of overidealization, interpersonal exploitiveness and devaluation and lack of empathy." and devaluation and lack of empathy."

Finally, the team observed,

> physically self-damaging acts; a pattern of unstable interpersonal relationships; an identity disturbance manifested by uncertainty about several issues relating to identity, namely self-image and career choice; and chronic feelings of emptiness or boredom; features of passive-aggressive personality disorder include resistance to parental demands for adequate performance for occupational and social functioning, combined with dawdling; . . . secretiveness; jealousy; overreaction to minor events; inability to sustain consistent work behavior; failure to accept social norms; lack of self-confidence; and several obsessive-compulsive traits.

Several reporters at the trial dubbed these traits "dementia suburbia."

Among the noteworthy sections of the report was one titled "Insight and Judgment":

> The defendant attributed his present difficulties to an "insane state of mind" brought about by the adverse influences upon him of various works of art and literature, the impact of current events, the failure of his treating psychiatrist (Dr. Hopper) to adequately diagnose and treat him, the pressure placed upon him by his parents to conform to middle class social

expectations, and numerous physical complaints. Additionally, Mr. Hinckley described himself as chronically depressed, anxious, alienated, and afflicted with a pervasive sense of poor self-esteem. He stated that he was unable to accept responsibility for the various failures in his life summarized above. His fundamental inability to relate the dynamics of his personality style to his significant problems emerged as the major deficit in the defendant's insight. Relatively simplistic formulations were promulgated to essentially exculpate himself from responsibility for his behaviors on March 30, 1981, and before.

The crucial section was called "Criminal Responsibility":

The following themes are among the most salient in the development of Mr. Hinckley's behavior eventuating in the shootings of March 30, 1981: repeated failure in social, educational, and occupational efforts; desire to achieve notoriety and fame; desire to gain the attention of Jodie Foster; the parental ultimatum; disappointment in the lack of immediate success of psychiatric treatment; and the failure of his identification with literary characters to produce personal satisfaction.

It is quite clear that these are not the reasonable acts of a completely rational individual. Our opinion about the legal question of criminal responsibility—and it is only an opinion, for the final determination is for the jury—does not hinge on psychiatric diagnoses or speculations. Mr. Hinckley's history is clearly indicative of a person who did not function in a usual, reasonable manner. However, there is no evidence that he was so impaired that he could not appreciate the wrongfulness of his conduct or conform his conduct to the requirements of the law.

Since the government's report was not admitted into evidence for the jury to consider, Dietz did not have to defend it or explain its logic. He used the report as a basis for his testimony, however, and his testimony was itself evidence for the jury to ponder. In it, Dietz concentrated on Hinckley's worst side; seen through Dietz's eyes, Hinckley became a lazy, fame-seeking, manipulative, self-concerned, and privileged loner, who harassed his parents about his inheritance, lied to them, and tricked them out of money. "The desire not to work can be traced back at least to the time after Mr. Hinckley's high-school graduation," Dietz declared. "I think that Mr. Hinkley's interest in the Beatles is the earliest sign that I've been able to discern that he became exceedingly interested in fame, in the notion of success, in fame in a way that would not require a great deal of effort." His concern with "art and literature" (Dietz's code words for a slick, violent movie and a lot of pulp books) grew from his obsession with fame. Hinckley, said Dietz, had spent the year before March 30th, 1981, choosing among "high-publicity crimes"—a phrase Dietz repeated with care: "He hadn't been occupationally successful. That is why he had to turn to high-publicity crime." Dietz reminded his audience that, on the night of the shooting, Hinckley had asked if the Academy Awards would still be televised, or if his deed would push them off the air. In an interview, Hinckley told Dietz, "The setup was so unbelievably perfect," when he went to the Washington Hilton. Dietz asked Hinckley if he had succeeded on March 30th. Hinckley, Dietz recounted, had smiled and answered, "Yeah, it worked." The defendant had gone on, "You know, actually, I accomplished everything I was going for there. Actually, I should feel good because I accomplished everything on a grand scale. Actually, I accomplished exactly what I wanted to accomplish without exception." "I didn't get any big thrill out of killing—I mean shooting—him," Hinckley confessed; "I did it for her sake. . . . The movie isn't over yet." In the doctor's view, the defendant's goal of impressing Jodie Foster "was indeed reasonable because he accomplished it." During a break in the testimony, Hinckley glowered and appeared to swear at Dietz.

Differences between the testimony of Carpenter and Dietz brought to mind Judge Bazelon's 1974 revision of his 1954 opinion: "My experience has shown that in no case is it more difficult to elicit productive and reliable expert testimony than in cases that call on the knowledge and practice of psychiatry." Carpenter's and Dietz's appearances were apparently productive and reliable, but the results of their testimony were contradictory. Instead of clarifying comments, they served up expert disagreement. Judge Bazelon had expected too much from psychiatrists. He had turned to psychiatrists for resolution of a social problem, and discovered they could not easily deliver within the constraints of a trial.

CHAPTER SEVEN

The Law
and
Psychiatry

DAVID BEAR, a psychiatrist for the defense, did his first brain research in high school. After graduating first in his class from Harvard College in 1965, Bear traveled the world on a fellowship, interviewing scientists who shared his interest in the brain and in human behavior. He attended Harvard Medical School, interned in neurology, studied psychiatry as a resident, and joined the faculty of his alma mater. At the time of Hinckley's trial, he taught psychiatry and directed a center for psychiatry and neurology. The prosecutor dubbed Bear "the Harvard doctor," although his witness, Park Dietz, was also associated with Harvard, as an assistant professor of psychiatry. (Dietz moved to the University of Virginia soon after the trial ended.) Nervous and inexperienced as a witness, Bear spoke like a reform candidate for Congress, but, his first day in court, he held the gallery fascinated with a primer on psychiatric diagnosis as a scientific method. He concluded that Hinckley suffered from a progressive illness he called schizophrenia spectrum disorder, and, at the time of the shooting, was in a major depressive episode which was made worse by an extreme reaction—"a paradoxical rage"—to Valium.

Bear also explained the meaning of schizophrenia, a state when thoughts split off from emotions and four abnormalities are usually present—blunted affect, when a person is perpetually as "cool as a cucumber"; ambivalence, when the person holds contradictory ideas at the same time; autism, or a retreat from the real world into a private one; and disjointed associations, when ideas do not flow in a logical pattern. Bear asked himself: Why Jodie Foster? What did she have to do with Hinckley shooting the President? Trying to think Hinckley's thoughts, Bear concluded that it was normal for a young man to fall in love with an actress, unusual for him to travel across country to see her, and even more unusual for him to try to talk with her. Jodie Foster "totally rejected" Hinckley. What was he to do? Men often try a telegram or flowers, Bear reasoned, and, if rejected again, "usually you lick your wound and go home." But Hinckley decided he had to "rescue" Jodie Foster, who was "a prisoner at Yale." "Every single time a psychiatrist sees thinking like that, every time, not as a matter of opinion, as a matter of fact, that is psychosis," Bear declared.

Where did Hinckley's ideas come from? In 1976, he repeatedly saw *Taxi Driver,* and cast himself as Travis Bickle, "a lonely, friendless, girlfriendless man," who was played by Robert De Niro. Hinckley, said Bear, felt "I am like Travis. I am a loner. I am unhappy. I have no girlfriend. I look around me. I see how horrible things are." Hinckley bought clothes like Travis's—an Army fatigue jacket, flannel shirts, and boots; he drank peach brandy, as Travis did; he kept a Travis-style diary. Travis fell for a political worker called Betsy, who was fine, blond, and accomplished; Hinckley invented Lynn Collins. Travis turned to guns, and so did Hinckley—he had to have three handguns, like

Travis, and play with them, posture with them, and pose in pictures with a gun to his head. Travis was a pill-taker and Hinckley became one; Travis met the child-prostitute Iris—played by Jodie Foster—befriended her, saw her as oppressed by pimps, and vowed to rescue her; Hinckley saw Jodie Foster as an innocent, trapped in society, a prisoner at Yale, and he vowed to liberate her.

At the judge's request, Bear summarized the plot of *Taxi Driver*, from memory. Travis Bickle arrives in New York City. He gets a job as a taxi-driver, cruises the city, and decides it is a lonely place. He yearns for a girlfriend, sees Betsy, meets her—and she shows interest. They go on a date and, out of inexperience, Travis takes her to a pornographic movie. She walks out on him, and he is heartbroken. He buys guns, and decides to "clean up the scum" in the city.

In a remarkable scene—which, said Bear, Hinckley remembered "as the most striking," and which Bear acted out on the stand—Travis stares into the camera, as if it were a mirror, and asks, "You talkin' to me? You talkin' to me? Well, I don't see anyone else here." According to Bear, Hinckley thought Travis was talking to him. Travis goes to kill the Presidential candidate Betsy works for, but the Secret Service spots him, and he runs. Iris has previously solicited him, and he's been horrified by the fact of a twelve-year-old prostitute. He decides to rescue her, and he shoots her pimp, the manager of the hotel where she turned tricks, and one of her customers. Travis is wounded in the attack. Out of bullets, he holds a finger to his head, clicks it repeatedly, and cracks, "This is the time for me to check out." The newspapers write up Travis as a hero. By chance, he picks up Betsy in his cab, and she shows interest in him again. To Bear, the message of the movie was disquieting: "Violence, horrible as it is, was rewarded." Hinckley "felt like he was acting out a movie script," Bear reported.

Hinckley's fantasies about Travis and Iris had taken over his mind.

The books found in Hinckley's hotel room the day of the shooting seemed to support Bear's diagnosis. From Nathaniel Benchley's *Welcome to Xanadu,* Hinckley took the idea of a kidnapping. (The book tells of a patient who escapes from a mental hospital, kidnaps a woman, takes her to an isolated cabin, wins her heart, and then kills himself when the police come to end the romance.) In a college report on the book, Hinckley translated its message: "Life can be whatever one makes it." In *The Fan,* Hinckley encountered a fictional hero who seeks a screen idol, scorns her, kills her, then kills himself. *The Fox Is Crazy Too*—a true story— has as its central figure Garrett Trapnell, who endures a sad and troubled childhood, later skyjacks a plane, and, at his trial, tries to feign insanity, although he really *is* mentally ill. Hinckley took the words of his hijack note, found in the Band-Aid box, from the note written and used by Trapnell.

Could Hinckley have faked his illness? When patients attempt this, according to Bear, they fake "positive" signs of schizophrenia, like hearing voices or seeing rays. Hinckley denied having these florid symptoms. The ones Bear noted were "negative," such as dried-up emotions or jumping thoughts. When Bear double-checked Hinckley's symptoms, "time after time his story was accurate." On the occasions Hinckley covered up, "distortion never made him look sicker." On March 30th, Hinckley saw three options: killing himself in Jodie Foster's presence in New Haven; shooting her, then shooting himself, in the style of *Romeo and Juliet;* and staying in Washington and shooting the President—to win Jodie Foster's love and admiration and "end the roller coaster of his agony." Could he have planned to shoot the President? "This is so much the heart of the issue," Bear emphasized. A logical man plans. Hinckley reacted to ideas of reference—"This is it! This is the signal!"—"the very opposite of logic." Bear declared, "Do I conclude he was rational in plan? My God, my sense of justice says absolutely not!"

At the end of the afternoon, Judge Parker excused the jury and asked Bear to testify on a question of evidence that had repeatedly been raised in legal papers and at bench conferences. As a tool of psychiatric diagnosis, he wondered, what was the value of a CAT-scan of the brain in this case? Short for "computerized axial tomography," a computer-enhanced, three-dimensional X-ray, the CAT-scan was a recent technological advance whose results, according to lawyers for both sides, had never been admitted as evidence in an American court. The session began with a rebuke.

JUDGE PARKER: You earlier had reference to what you considered to be your sense of justice.

DR. BEAR: Uh-huh.

JUDGE PARKER: Your sense of justice is not sought here. You are not to make that sort of statement before the jury.

As the judge implied, Bear's job was to provide expert opinion about John Hinckley's mental condition before and during the shooting. The blend of Hinckley's right to a trial by jury, the court's insistence on maintaining due process in the trial, and the jury's application of the District's laws to reach a verdict on Hinckley's criminal responsibility would express society's sense of justice.

Then Bear testified about the CAT-scan: "As an instrument for viewing the brain, I think it is absolutely unquestioned. It is considered the greatest diagnostic advance perhaps in the last fifty years. It is used routinely." The judge asked Bear to go further, and comment on the CAT-scan as a psychiatric tool. Could it help determine whether or not a person was responsible for his acts? As a psychiatrist who studied biology's lessons about human behavior, Bear was convinced that it could. There is "overwhelming evidence," he said, that the brain's physiology relates to a person's emotions and that an abnormal appearance of the brain relates to schizophrenia; and the scan is "a very powerful way of viewing the brain" that can show whether or not this abnormal appearance exists. The prosecutor asked Bear about the appearance he had in mind:

PROSECUTOR: Is it generally the accepted view of all psychiatrists that widened sulci [folds and ridges on the surface of the brain], as they are called, indicate the person suffering from that phenomenon has schizophrenia? Is that a unanimous view?

DR. BEAR: It is nobody's view.

PROSECUTOR: Isn't it true that the studies that you are talking about indicate that most people who are schizophrenic don't have widened sulci?

DR. BEAR: To be precise about the word "most": In one study from St. Elizabeths Hospital, one-third of the schizophrenics had widened sulci. That is a high figure. It is true that the simple majority didn't . . . but the fact that one-third had these widened sulci—whereas in normals, probably less than one out of fifty have them—that is a very powerful fact.

PROSECUTOR: That is a fact?

DR. BEAR: Yes. Yes. It is a statistical fact. . . . It is as much a fact as this: We know statistically that a male who smokes ten to twenty packs of cigarettes is twenty times more likely to get lung cancer. That is a fact and it is a strong enough fact for the Surgeon General to write on the package, "Don't smoke." Yet it is very clear nobody can say that anyone who takes the next cigarette will get lung cancer. It is a statistical fact, as I mentioned, that one-third of schizophrenics have widened sulcis and probably less than two per cent of normal people have them. That is a powerful statistical fact and it would bear on the opinion in this case.

The judge excused Dr. Bear from the courtroom, and heard arguments from counsel about whether the jury should be allowed to consider the results of John Hinckley's CAT-scan. The defense framed its interests in limited terms: Hinckley's scans showed widened sulci—evidence of his shrunken brain; these occur more frequently in schizophrenics than in normal men his age; his widened sulci were not the cause of his schizophrenia, but, following a clinical diagnosis of schizophrenia by several doctors, the widened sulci "substantially increased the likelihood" that Hinckley was schizophrenic. The government argued that there was no sound evidence that a CAT-scan could aid diagnosis of schizophrenia and, further, a CAT-scan could not corroborate Hinckley's schizophrenia since no such schizophrenia had been proved. Witnesses for the prosecution compared the evidence to other false leads about schizophrenia, such as a link between double Y chromosomes in human cells and violent behavior. While the government recognized the promise of the CAT-scan and the contribution it had already made to medicine through its pictures of tumors and other brain problems, it maintained that there were no grounds for admitting Hinckley's CAT-scans. The judge showed little interest in a thorough presentation, and he ruled that he would not "at this point" admit Hinckley's scan or testimony about it. Nine days later, after the defense team rounded out its expert testimony, the judge heard a day of further argument about the CAT-scan, again ruled it inadmissible, and then changed his mind over the weekend. A fortnight after David Bear addressed the issue, the judge let the defense present Hinckley's scan to the jury, adding a new page to the history of evidence.

When Bear left the stand after testifying about the CAT-scan, he knew none of this. Bear went back to his hotel and called a colleague in Toronto to check on the progress of a conference he was missing. The colleague did what he shouldn't have done: he told Bear what he had heard on the news—that the judge had ruled against admission of the CAT-scan. Bear didn't know the judge's ruling was not final and, as a witness still under oath, he was not supposed to talk with anyone about the case. But he knew how important the scan was to his own analysis of Hinckley's case. As a scientist, he was angered by the judge's conservatism and what he viewed as the government's anti-intellectual stance. Using a statistical measure called Bayes' theorem, Bear had concluded that the CAT-scan showed there was a 94 percent probability that Hinckley was schizophrenic. Here was tangible evidence of Hinckley's disorder, something the defendant could not fake, and the court would not allow the jury to see it.

Bear slept badly. In the morning, he went to the courthouse for his second day of testimony and picked up breakfast at a basement cafeteria. He was considering what to do, when he recognized a marshal from the Hinckley courtroom and, without talking specifics, asked what the marshal thought of his visiting the judge in chambers to raise an extraordinary question. The marshal discouraged him. Judge John Sirica, a senior trial judge whose bravery while presiding at the Watergate trials impressed Bear, came by, and the marshal introduced the doctor to the judge. Bear didn't mention his quandary to the judge, but merely talking with Sirica emboldened him to make an unusual move when he returned to the courtroom.

Back on the stand, at the start of cross-examination, Bear interrupted Judge Parker, to request the right to speak with John Hinckley's counsel. Off his guard, then perturbed, Judge Parker excused the jury and lectured Bear, calling his request "foreign to this situation." Bear insisted on being heard. "I need the advice of counsel about what facts I may use in my answer," he said. "I need guidance, very careful guidance." The judge asked Bear to step off the witness stand and called the defense lawyers to his bench. "What is wrong with this man this morning?" he asked. Hinckley's lawyers guessed that Bear was uncertain how much he could say about the CAT-scan or about John Hinckley's suicide attempts after the March 30th shooting. In May of 1981 and again in November, first by an overdose of Tylenol tablets, then by hanging, Hinckley had tried to kill himself. Both sides treated the events gingerly, the defense because evidence of them could be ruled prejudicial, the prosecution because attempts at suicide might seem to confirm Hinckley's lack of balance. When Bear resumed the stand, the judge ordered him not to refer to the CAT-scans or the attempts. Bear was still not satisfied, and gave a long explanation of his position. "My guidance as a witness, my responsibility, comes from the Washington instruction," he began, referring to an instruction for expert witnesses, set forth in a post-Durham case called Washington *v*. United States.

> I believe that I am not able to complete the responsibilities as a witness under the Washington instruction because the Washington instruction clearly advises me to testify as to my clinical judgment, first of a mental condition, not using legal terms, but medical terms, and it advises me to present my conclusion to the jury using the observations and the medical tests that I would routinely use in evaluating a patient. I would routinely order the CAT-scan and use it to evaluate Mr. Hinckley, to advise his family about the outcome. Furthermore, it is my expert opinion that at the majority of universities every complete evaluation of Mr. Hinckley would include the CAT-scan and that, in fact, the government's agreement that one performs CAT-scans on Hinckley is their acknowledgement that this is part of a full exam. I therefore reach the following conclusions. Either I'm not able to proceed to testify as an expert witness, as the Washington rule directs me,

or I would like the right to state to the jury that an important test which I use in reaching my conclusions has been barred by the court and I was not able to present it to the jury, though I believe it would influence their decision as it has influenced mine. If not, under the law and my obligations, I am not able to continue as an expert witness. I could not answer a single question.

Along with everyone else in the room, the judge was stunned. "Well, doctor," he managed, "you really have gone to great lengths." Undeterred, the doctor continued:

If I cannot present the complete facts, I have not fulfilled the terms of this rule, and, your honor, I say this with great respect, the fact that the attorneys choose to ask questions about the CAT-scan at this point in time is not an accurate reflection of my diagnostic thinking. I, at the beginning of the examination, I knew from day one that a CAT-scan would be absolutely essential. I do not view it as ancillary. I view it as one of a number of findings. But I do not view it as coming last. That was merely a convenience in order of presentation, so I would not accept the conclusion that this was a final, added, and in some ways unimportant piece of evidence. To me, it is a very important piece of evidence, and I have not fulfilled my role as an expert unless I report it.

Bear's moment of conscience ended. After another bench conference, to discuss striking the doctor's testimony altogether, and a half-hour recess, to give Hinckley's red-faced lawyers the chance to remind Bear of his proper role at trial, he was amenable to cross-examination. When he returned to the stand, Bear looked chastened, but he showed little tolerance for the prosecutor's queries. The outburst had changed him from a young and gifted professor ("the son-in-law every Jewish mother wants for her daughter," one observer called him) to a determined pedant, his furies unleashed. The prosecutor baited him and Bear quibbled, his manner arrogant and unyielding. To the jury, the change must have been confusing. They had sat through a crisp presentation the day before, been excused for a few hours in the morning, and, after they returned, watched a man now swept by strong, mysterious, emotional currents.

Hinckley's CAT-scans—the court eventually permitted the defense to show two, one taken soon after the shooting, the other a year later—accomplished less than the defense would have liked, and less than the government had feared. After weeks of legal wrangling, and his ultimate decision to admit the scans, the judge did all he could to neutralize his decision. He refused to dim the courtroom lights during the display, and he insisted that the slides of Hinckley's scans be projected on a small screen set up across the large room from the jury. The performance had the impact of a short, poorly rehearsed, and annoying farce. In washed-out colors, the scans looked like slices of bruised and misshapen fruit. Clutching a yard-long stick, the radiologist who pointed out what was "strikingly abnormal" about the scans made the presentation even stranger. She shuffled to the screen in slippers and spoke in a trembling voice. By the end of the interlude, it was not likely that anyone in court had seen the scans as the clincher, closing the case with final proof of John Hinckley's disorder.

Besides Carpenter and Bear, the defense put on two other major witnesses. Ernst Prelinger, a psychologist from Yale University, looked like a retired college president, still handsome, with watchful eyes and swept-back hair. The narrow end of his tie hung below the wide one, and he wore a big silver belt buckle with the imprint of a whale. In a Viennese accent, Prelinger presented results from Hinckley's psychological tests. On the Wechsler Adult Intelligence Scale, Hinckley's overall I.Q. registered 113, which put him in the eightieth percentile, or in the category of bright normal. On the Minnesota Multiphasic Personality Inventory, the most commonly used test in forensic psychology, Hinckley achieved a remarkable score. The test consisted of five hundred and fifty statements requiring an answer of true or false. The statements included:

I believe I am being plotted against.
I believe I am being followed.
There is something wrong with my mind.
I wish I could be as happy as others seem to be.

The test was scored on a dozen scales, three of which screened for intentional distortion and nine of which indicated various mental abnormalities, from hypochondriasis to depression, hysteria, and schizophrenia. Hinckley's test results showed he was not faking; on all but one scale, for hypomania, his scores reached high peaks, far above the usual line between normal and abnormal. Prelinger said the chance of Hinckley's score not indicating serious problems was one in a million. On one measure, for depression, Hinckley's score climbed almost to the summit of the chart for abnormality.

Thomas Goldman, a young, lean, and low-keyed forensic psychiatrist from Washington, sat as the final expert for the defense. The prosecutor gave Goldman a difficult afternoon. After seamless testimony, during which he called Hinckley "an errant child"—one "who had done something bad, not terribly, not unspeakably awful, something bad for which he is sorry now and he feels he ought to be forgiven"—Goldman let a thread show. He did not know how many bullets Hinckley had in his hotel room before the shooting, and he did not know how many of them were Devastators that exploded on impact, causing even more damage than normal bullets. He knew only what Hinckley had told him: by chance, his gun was loaded with Devastators. The prosecutor pounced:

Q: Doctor, let me tell you the evidence in this case shows that the man had thirty-seven other bullets and six Devastator bullets before he loaded the gun. When he loaded the gun, he put six bullets of Devastator type in the gun and no other, right?

A: Yes, sir.

Q: And he left no Devastator bullets in his room. In other words he put all six in the gun?

A: I see.

Q: Having told you that and informed you of that, do you still believe him when he claimed he put the Devastator bullets in at random and by accident?

A: No.

Q: He lied to you, didn't he?

A: That is a reasonable inference.

Q: A fact, doctor.

A: As he told me about it relatively early in the game, yes, but I think you may very well be right, that he lied about that.

Q: It is a fact that he lied, doctor; it is not an inference at all, is it?

In a tactical shift, the government reduced its list of experts from five (besides Dietz, they included forensic psychiatrists Jonas Rappeport and James Cavanaugh, and neurologist Ernst Rodin) to two, closing with Sally Johnson, the court-appointed doctor who interviewed Hinckley for a longer time than any other psychiatrist. Twenty-nine years old, her brown hair in a tight bun, Dr. Johnson spent almost as much time on the stand as Dietz, winning the gallery with a concerned smile and perseverance. One spectator, who came almost every day and said he thought he was a lot like John Hinckley ("All my friends say I'm a loner," he confessed, smiling) liked Sally Johnson's "cute" voice. Of all the witnesses, Sally Johnson managed a unique combination: she seemed sympathetic, while what she said was censorious. She also used a mix of psychiatric language and colloquial phrases. To explain why Hinckley was vague, she said, "I think that the reason was . . . that he didn't at that point in the evaluation want to present himself as somebody who was real together and around that time capable of any type of planning."

At the start of Dr. Johnson's testimony, Hinckley waved to her and watched, with his own sort of enthusiasm, apparently to see if she really liked him—that was the question he wanted his lawyers to ask her. At the end, when her position could not be mistaken, he gave her the same glare he had trained on Dietz, mouthing obscenities. In between, Johnson told how Hinckley had known the names of assassins like Lee Harvey Oswald, James Earl Ray, Sirhan Sirhan, and Arthur Bremer; how he was pleased that his name had gone from "totally nothing" to publication in thousands of newspapers; how he had a swollen sense of self-importance; and how he suffered from personality disorders, with narcissistic and mixed (schizoid, borderline, and passive-aggressive) features. The personality disorders were not normal and not psychotic; they did not, she said, prevent Hinckley from being responsible for his actions on March 30th. Johnson also revealed in court that she didn't believe Hinckley shot the President to win Jodie Foster's love; breaking courtroom decorum, Hinckley retorted, "You're wrong!" Finally, she reported what Hinckley recalled for her about the shooting, the first time they met, on April 3rd, 1981: Just before pulling the trigger, he thought, "I'll never have a better opportunity."

Except for evidence about the CAT-scan, a complete showing of *Taxi Driver* closed the case for the defense. The television sets were moved back into position and, in the light of the courtroom, the movie's colors were dark and brooding. The feature's blue jazz and monologues by a sleepless Robert De Niro sounded close, intimate, unnerving. Jodie Foster wore a floppy hat, oversize sunglasses, and towering platform shoes. Comic, gap-toothed, and cheery, the baby-faced prostitute she played was an unlikely inspiration for Hinckley's deeds. A weird, disturbing sequence of violence brought the movie quickly to an end.

In final arguments, which summarized the evidence for both sides, the prosecution and the defense distilled into a day and a half the styles and contentions they had rehearsed over the preceding seven weeks of trial. For the government, Roger Adelman offered a nasty, detailed, and brilliant summary of the shooting, as if John Hinckley's were a sensational murder trial, without an insanity defense. "He said, 'I'll never have a better opportunity,' " Adelman began, asking the jury to review the evidence. He reminded them of the impact of the bullets on Delahanty's back and Brady's brain, and the sequence of the shots. The prosecutor badgered: If Hinckley had been out of control, would he have hit four people with six shots? In his summary, Adelman also skewered the defense witnesses. "With all of these degrees . . . that Dr. Bear received, you didn't hear him tell you that he got one for common sense," he observed. Dr. Goldman believed that Hinckley chose the bullets for the shooting at random; Dr. Prelinger saw Hinckley only twice; and, in Adelman's version, Dr. Carpenter suggested to Hinckley that his victims were "bit players" in his delusional life. "That's an outrageous thought," Adelman shouted, too loud for the courtroom, "that the President of the United States and a man shot in the brain are 'bit players.' " What was Hinckley's insanity defense? Four types of schizophrenia, Valium, *Taxi Driver*, Jodie Foster, CAT-scans, John Lennon:"A *smorgasbord*"—he had "so many claims he really doesn't have any at all." John Hinckley had "a very good upbringing" and a sad life and he followed Jodie Foster "just like any other young man with a fantasy." Dr. Hopper "didn't blow it" when he had Hinckley in treatment: "That's John Hinckley's rationalization. . . . John Hinckley doesn't want to take the responsibility." Adelman sneered, "He is not charged here with being sad at Christmas. He is not charged here with going to the Dakota apartment building in New York in February. He is not even charged here with stalking President Carter in Nashville or President Carter out in Dayton. He is charged with 13 crimes that happened at 2:20 P.M. on the 30th of March."

The government doctors, Adelman reminded, found that Hinckley had the capacity to take responsibility. Dr. Dietz was "careful, thorough, complete, and . . . very fair," and he concluded that Hinckley had a "strong desire for fame." Dr. Johnson, who spent more time with Hinckley in 1981 than his parents did and knew him better than any of the other doctors, made an independent diagnosis and agreed with the conclusion of the government's team. John Hinckley was "an ordinary person" who had been "put under a microscope," but he knew what he was doing on March 30th. "I'm sure you can imagine the word 'kill' going through his mind. You don't have to imagine it. In the letter to Jodie Foster he wrote about his attempt to 'get Reagan.'" The hour of the shooting, Adelman surmised, "He's thinking about killing." The prosecutor concluded, "It all comes back to what John Hinckley said. He said, speaking of himself with gun in hand up there at the Hilton, 'I will never have a better opportunity.'"

Vincent Fuller, head of the defense's legal team, acknowledged the "tragic shooting of four innocent victims" but stressed that the "indictment . . . is uncontested, except as to one issue." The government's evidence was full of "highly emotionally charged documents" but they did not "reflect upon the defendant's mental state and upon his legal responsibility." Fuller also had words, some of them pointed, for each of the government's witnesses. Of the government's doctors, Fuller said, "I think they . . . trivialized the frenetic behavior of the defendant." In Fuller's view, Hinckley was "emotionally deprived for a period of at least seven years prior to his being interviewed by Sally Johnson." With her, "he wanted to put a good light on himself." Fuller didn't mean to be "critical," but Dr. Johnson had only two years of forensic experience when she interviewed Hinckley, and Dr. Dietz only four.

The defense case, on the other hand, did not rely on doctors alone, Fuller argued. Evidence from Hinckley's family, medical doctors, his writings, and experts in mental health showed "the gradual deterioration of the human mind over a period of many years." From high school on, he reminded the jury, Hinckley had no friends. His only experience of the world came in fast-food places, supermarkets, or airports on his travels. By 1980, he was obsessed with Jodie Foster, with no hope of a relationship. Waving his arms, Fuller read from Hinckley's New Year's Eve monologue: " 'John Lennon is dead, the world is over, forget it. . . . It's just going to be insanity if I even make it through the first few days.' " Fuller went on. Soon after this, Dr. Hopper set unrealistic goals for Hinckley (having a job by the start of March and being out of his parents' house by the end of the month). At the same time, Hinckley contemplated his own unrealistic goals—suicide, or killing Jodie Foster, or both. "To what end?" Fuller asked. "To gain the love and admiration and establish a relationship with a woman. It's delusional thinking," he snapped contemptuously. "That's all it is, pure and simple. It's pathetic, but it's delusional."

For most of Fuller's presentation, Hinckley sat with his

eyes hidden by his hand. Toward the end, his shoulders dropped and his face grew mottled. Gregory Craig served as Fuller's junior partner in the defense; throughout the trial, when he was not questioning witnesses, Craig sat next to Hinckley as his confidant and counselor. Fuller had rarely talked to the defendant in the courtroom. Craig and Hinckley whispered to each other often, and passed notes. When Hinckley chewed on his tie, aped the sketch artists who stared at him through opera glasses by making an imaginary pair with his hands and gawking back, or otherwise acted up, Craig brought him into line. On some days, they wore similar tan suits. Sandy-haired, with cheeks whose glow defied the two months of trial indoors, Craig appeared full of promise. Hinckley's bloom had gone. During Fuller's summation, Craig doodled on a yellow pad. He noticed Hinckley's slump, shifted closer to his charge, and put his hand on Hinckley's arm. The top half of Hinckley's face didn't move beneath a stream of tears, but his jaw and mouth quivered. Judge Parker watched Hinckley from the bench and signaled for a marshal to take him out, but the marshal missed the sign. In full voice, Fuller argued on about Jodie Foster and John Hinckley. Gregory Craig held Hinckley's arm, and saw him cry for the first time in the fifteen months they had known each other.

CHAPTER EIGHT

The Adams Closing

ABOUT FIFTY DAYS after the sanity verdict in the Adams case (and a week before the Hinckley verdict) Judge Moultrie held a hearing, required by law, to determine if Rufus Adams should be committed to St. Elizabeths Hospital, where he had been under evaluation for fifty days, or if he should be sentenced to prison on the five counts for which he had been found guilty. Except for the judge, lawyers for the government and for the defense, the defendant, and the judge's usual retinue—a law clerk, a court clerk, and a couple of marshals—the courtroom was almost empty. The hearing required no jury, and had attracted few spectators. Two doctors from St. Elizabeths, one black, the other white, had submitted a joint report to the court stating that Rufus Adams was no longer a danger to himself or society because of a mental disease or defect. One doctor called Adams alert, cooperative, punctual, and expressive, with no delusional thinking, hallucinations, or defects in judgment. In his view, the defendant was merely antisocial, with a "maladaptive way of dealing with the environment." The other doctor added that Adams had "compulsive and narcissistic features." The defendant was dangerous, in his view, but not as a result of a mental disease or defect. In effect, the government doctors recommended that Rufus Adams should be sentenced to a term in prison, not treated at St. Elizabeths.

At the end of the hearing, the judge asked Gary Kohlman, the defense counsel, if he had anything further to add. "Yes, Your Honor, unfortunately there is a lot further," Kohlman said at the start of an unusual speech that came out as a harangue. "As far as I'm concerned, this proceeding is standing a whole series of principles on their head and essentially making a mockery of both the trial that we had and the conclusion that was reached by the jury." He continued, "We were perfectly satisfied with Mr. Adams being in the hospital and getting treatment. There is not a scintilla of doubt that, had the jury returned verdicts of not guilty by reason of insanity on all the counts, that, A, the Saint Elizabeths Hospital would never have been making a recommendation that the gentleman be released into the community, and, B, that the government, in a million years, would not be going along with it, even if Saint Elizabeths made that recommendation.

"As I see this proceeding, we, the defense, have the burden of proving to Your Honor that Mr. Adams is no longer a danger to the community by virtue of mental illness. We have, as impetus behind that, a jury verdict that on the day of the offenses, at least, Mr. Adams was mentally ill and that one of these offenses was a product of mental illness." He went on, "A man with this record would be laughed out of court if the defense ever came in fifty days after a verdict like this and tried to get him released. Yet because the government knows and Saint Elizabeths knows that this person also has a sentence to serve," they recommend as they did.

Kohlman asked that Adams be committed to Saint Eliza-beths, for the "treatment the community believes he needs."

The judge responded, making no effort to hide his anger. "Before I ask the government to respond, let me say this, Mr. Kohlman. The court may consider your request, but it would not consider it on the basis that you concluded," he said. "That would be an indictment of the medical staff, which this court will not be in a position to adopt. That would be an effrontery to the medical staff, if this court were to permit a continuation of a case on that premise."

Steven Gordon, in rebuttal, called the St. Elizabeths staff "very professional" and chastised Kohlman for proposing "too many 'what if's.'" "The verdict is in the past," Gordon reminded the court, and Kohlman was trying to evade the hospital's conclusion: "Rufus Adams is dangerous, but not as a result of any disorder." The judge wrapped up the hearing. "The court admits this is a peculiar situation, but can still reach a conclusion," he said, announcing his agreement with the recommendation from St. Elizabeths. Referring to a formal plea for leniency, he concluded, "Counsel can present any allocution at sentencing."

On the way out of the local courthouse, across a plaza from the federal building where John Hinckley was still on trial, Kohlman snapped his fingers, smiled wryly, and wondered out loud if he had done the right thing. Noting that out of three hundred insanity acquittees evaluated by St. Elizabeths in the past fifteen years, Rufus Adams was only the second whom the hospital had not committed, Kohlman said, "I think I had to do it," and added, "but there's no question I was hoist by my own petard."

CHAPTER NINE

The
Verdict

THE HINCKLEY TRIAL came quickly to an end after the government's rebuttal, but the coda stretched over a weekend and into the next evening. On Friday, June 18, Judge Parker read the jury a dozen pages of instructions, including the Brawner rule, a definition of mental disease ("any abnormal condition of the mind, regardless of its medical label, which substantially affects mental or emotional processes and substantially impairs his behavior controls"), and a reminder that there had to be a "causal relationship between the disease and the unlawful act" for the jury to find John Hinckley insane. Two instructions stood out. The first, which concerned burden of proof as applied in federal cases, read: "The burden is on the Government to prove beyond a reasonable doubt either that the defendant was not suffering from a mental disease or defect on March 30, 1981, or else that he nevertheless had substantial capacity on that date both to conform his conduct to the requirements of the law and to appreciate the wrongfulness of his conduct. If the Government has not established this to your satisfaction beyond a reasonable doubt, then you shall bring a verdict of not guilty by reason of insanity." Three of the thirteen counts against Hinckley were federal, including assault on a federal officer, use of a firearm during commission of a felony, and the attempted assassination of the President. In local court, the burden of proof would have been on the defense to prove Hinckley's insanity. Judge Parker rejected the prosecution's request that the jury be bound by the local rule for the local crimes and the federal rule for the others, and ruled that, in this federal court, he would give the federal rule for the full indictment. The second key instruction was called "Effect of a Finding of Not Guilty by Reason of Insanity." With no inflection in his voice, the judge read: "If the defendant is found not guilty by reason of insanity it becomes the duty of the court to commit him to St. Elizabeths Hospital. There will be a hearing within fifty days to determine whether the defendant is entitled to be released. In that hearing the defendant has the burden of proof. The defendant will remain in custody, and will be entitled to release from custody only if the court finds by a preponderance of the evidence that he is not likely to injure himself or other persons due to mental illness."

During the trial, the dozen regular jurors and six alternates could take no notes (after four days of trial, the judge considered, then discarded the notion) and they were not supposed to talk about the case, even with each other. Although the *Washington Post* featured the trial daily and the local television and radio stations often led the news with the story, the jurors were told to disregard the coverage. In theory, the jurors discussed the trial for the first time when they began to deliberate, late on Friday afternoon. By occupation, the jurors described themselves as a food-service technician, a custodian, a secretary, a banquet houseman, a supply specialist, a shop mechanic, an information-control clerk, another secretary, a garage attendant, and a research assistant; two were retired. Four worked for the government, six for private firms. All but one were black. They averaged thirty-nine years of age, with three in their twenties, four in their thirties, two in their forties, another fifty, and two more in their sixties. At sixty-four, the first foreman chosen was the oldest juror. The group threw names in his hat—the only one available—and he picked out his own. But after two and a half days, he "declined the burden of that responsibility," as he wrote in a note to the judge, and the youngest juror, at twenty-two, took over. The jurors sent a few other notes to the judge, asking for transcripts of the parents' testimony (declined) and of Dr. Carpenter's on Hinckley's "formative years" (declined), a list of evidence (granted), a stapler (granted), and a dictionary to look up definitions of "poetry" and "fiction" (declined). They also moved from the jury room back into the spacious courtroom for deliberation when they realized how many documents they had to review.

On Monday evening, soon after the jury returned to its regular chamber from an early supper, security at the door of the courtroom tightened up. JoAnn and Jack Hinckley arrived at seven-fifteen, and, a half hour later, in his tan suit, John Hinckley entered the courtroom, accompanied by marshals. Hinckley tapped his fingers on the table and whispered to Gregory Craig. Judge Parker took the bench and confirmed that the jury had reached a verdict at six-twenty that evening. He asked the defendant to stand. The young, black foreman of the jury gave the judge the written verdict and the judge silently flipped through it, noting the findings on thirteen separate counts. The judge then read it aloud, in an angry rush: "As to count one"—and all the others —"not guilty by reason of insanity." Hinckley crossed his hands in front of him, rocking on his heels, took a deep breath, and slowly nodded his head. JoAnn Hinckley cried out, clutched her husband, then composed herself; Jack stared at the bench in front of him, with a fist in front of his mouth. The defense lawyers shook hands. Roger Adelman puffed his cheeks, and unstacked, then re-piled the materials in front of him. When the gallery stirred, the judge snarled at a marshal, "Mr. Marshal, if you can't keep order there, get someone who can." As if Hinckley had been convicted and not acquitted, the judge set a "sentencing" date and then, correcting himself, remanded the defendant to St. Elizabeths. For the first time during the long and often bloodless trial, the court's overhead lights were not lit, and the room was subdued in a dim glow, like dusk. The final session took eight minutes.

CHAPTER TEN

Aftermath

JOHN HINCKLEY had expected to be convicted. The day before the jury brought in its verdict, he composed a speech to be read at his sentencing.

> God does indeed work in mysterious ways. My life has be-
> come a melodrama. My past has been studied and analyzed
> not only by psychiatrists but by a large part of the general
> public. I am now a household name. It has to be pure and
> simple fate that these things have happened to me. From the
> start, all I wanted was for someone to love me. I desperately
> wanted to be loved but I never could give appropriate love in
> return. I seem to have a need to hurt those people that I love
> the most. This is true in relation to my family and to Jodie
> Foster. I love them so much but I have this compulsion to
> destroy them. On March 30, 1981 I was asking my family
> to take me back and I was asking Jodie Foster to hold me in
> her heart. My assassination attempt was an act of love. I'm
> sorry love has to be so painful.

In the days after the verdict of acquittal, the jurors might have felt like Vietnam veterans, returning to a country that expressed a contempt for its soldiers instead of fury over a long war. Lawrence Coffey, the young foreman, sat on his front stoop and, to clusters of reporters, struggled to explain why the jury had reached its verdict. "The prosecutor's evidence was not strong enough," he concluded. George Blyther, another juror, told why the jury had not pronounced Hinckley "guilty but insane." "We weren't lawmakers," he reminded. "We had to give a judgment back the way it was given to us. The evidence being what it was, we were required to send John back insane." A couple of jurors broke ranks. Although the verdict had to have been unanimous, Nathalia Brown and Maryland Copelin called a press conference to say they had been pressured into an acquittal. "I felt I was on the brink of insanity myself going through this," Brown complained. The foreman and the dissenters joined two others in an unusual appearance before the Senate Subcommittee on Criminal Law. Senator Arlen Specter, Republican of Pennsylvania, presided, and afterward reported that he and other senators thought the jurors did not understand the instructions Judge Parker had given them. Miffed by comments that the jury had focused on Hinckley's mental illness and not on his criminal responsibility, Belinda Drake, a juror who was not at the Senate hearing, told the *Washington Post* that she and the others had understood their job, and had done it with particular fairness, as only a black jury (there was one white member) could.

Within a month, committees of the House and Senate plunged into hearings on the insanity defense. Henry Steadman, the mental-health researcher from New York State, put the defense in statistical perspective for the legislators. In 1978 (there are no up-to-date data), there were 1,625 insanity acquittals in the United States, ranging from none in Delaware, Iowa, North Dakota, South Dakota, West Virginia, and Wyoming to 169 in California. There were no available national statistics on the total number of insanity pleas entered, but one study reported one acquittal in 102 pleas—less than one percent—between 1970 and 1972 in Wyoming; and 86 acquittals in 458 pleas—nineteen percent—between 1969 and 1975 in Hawaii. The Public Advocate of New Jersey backed up Steadman's numbers. "All empirical analyses . . . have been consistent," he testified. "The public, the legal profession, and specifically legislators dramatically and grossly overestimate both the frequency and the success rate of the insanity defense."

Who wins insanity acquittals? At the start of the trial, according to an Associated Press/NBC News poll, eighty-seven percent of a public sample believed that too many murderers were using insanity pleas to avoid jail. Edwin Meese, as Counselor to the President, shared this view. In a speech against the insanity defense, he insisted, "We would do a lot better as far as ridding the streets of some of the most dangerous people that are out there." In fact, the nature of the crime seems to bear less on a court's decision than the findings of the psychiatric report, which gives special weight to psychosis. "Basically," Dr. Steadman concluded, "what the clinicians recommend, the court does." Although in New York and Michigan insanity verdicts most frequently followed charges of murder, manslaughter, assault, and arson, the crimes for which defendants were acquitted varied widely; offenses like forgery, shoplifting, car theft, and other forms of larceny filled out a long list and, in some jurisdictions, Steadman testified, they represented the "vast majority" of crimes for which defendants were found not guilty by reason of insanity. (In 1982 in New Jersey, only three of fifteen successful insanity defendants, or twenty percent, had committed homicides; in Missouri and Oregon, five percent had.) "In contrast to public perceptions and media portrayals," Dr. Steadman reported, "all insanity acquittees are not assassins, rapists, deranged mutilators, or mass murderers." In New York, the average hospital stay for an acquitted insanity defendant was three and a half years, and almost a third who were still hospitalized had been in for more than seven years; in New Jersey, insanity acquittees were generally confined to maximum-security hospitals for twice as long as the average prison term for a convicted felon. In both states, murderers and rapists spent more time hospitalized than burglars and car thieves. After three years, about three-fourths of both the insanity acquittees and the convicted felons were released in New York. Recidivism rates were somewhat lower for insanity acquittees than for convicted felons, and higher than for patients released from state civil hospitals.

Many members of Congress did not seem interested in this perspective. The insanity defense was important as a symbol of criminal justice, they said, and if the public misperceived it, then the Congress had to change the ground rules. In twenty-six bills introduced soon after the Hinckley verdict to limit the defense, the sponsors ignored the fact that most insanity defenses take place in state rather than federal courts, so that a federal law on the insanity defense (and it would be the first passed, aside from the special act of Congress in 1970 including an insanity law for the District of Columbia) might have value as a model, but would directly affect the lives of few defendants. A few months after the Hinckley verdict, and following a one-time survey of the ninety-four U.S. Attorneys' offices around the country, the Justice Department revealed that, in 1981, "only four federal defendants were acquitted of charges on the basis of a successful insanity defense": two people charged with bank robbery, one with murder, and one with making a threat by mail.

The least controversial of the Congressional recommendations for reform in a new federal statute came from Senator Arlen Specter, of Pennsylvania, who proposed that the legislature shift the burden of proof of insanity in federal cases from the prosecution, where the Supreme Court had placed it in 1895, to the defense. Before the Hinckley verdict, about half the states placed the burden to prove insanity on the defense. By 1984, the fraction increased to two-thirds. Supporters of this shift argued that the burden of proof was particularly important when the question was as subjective as a defendant's sanity, and suggested that placing the burden on the prosecution, while traditional in criminal cases, was unfair in insanity cases, because complex psychiatric testimony makes it too easy to raise a reasonable doubt about sanity. In Hollywood, soon after the Hinckley verdict, President Reagan illustrated his view about burden of proof in typical down-home fashion: "If you start thinking about even a lot of your friends, you would have to say, 'Gee, if I had to prove they were sane, I would have a hard job.'" Edwin Meese gave a similar example, substituting White House staff members for the President's friends.

In 1967, the President's Commission on Crime in the District of Columbia, where the burden of proof lay on the prosecution in both federal and local trials, recommended against a change. The Commission reported that the prosecution had not encountered difficulty in meeting the burden of proof; it argued that a shift would be unfair to the "indigent accused," and might "require substantial public expenditures to provide independent psychiatrists and other experts for indigent defendants." In 1970, in the District's special act on the insanity defense, the Congress shifted the burden of proof to the defense. Although the law explicitly directs that it shall be applied to federal as well as local trials, federal judges have ignored the provision. They continue to place the burden of proof of insanity on the prosecution, following the Supreme Court's nineteenth-century opinion. Local judges, on the other hand, heeded the decade-old statute, placing the burden on the defense. Until the Hinckley case, many District lawyers assumed that juries ignored the legal burden anyway, using common sense to balance conflicting arguments and decide the fates of defendants. But during the month after the Hinckley verdict, the government earnestly considered taking an extraordinary appeal from the verdict, on the grounds that Judge Parker had wrongly instructed the jury about burden of proof by ignoring the burden-shifting statute. The U.S. Attorney formally recommended the appeal; attorneys in the Solicitor General's office found only a narrow legal basis for the claim, noted the political risks of prolonging the case, and advised against it. Accepting their counsel, the Attorney General decided not to challenge the verdict.

A proposal for an optional verdict, "guilty but mentally ill," also provoked heated national debate. The idea won wide support, with no one single champion. As an alternative to the traditional insanity verdict, the finding implies that someone who satisfies the strictest standard of mental illness and insanity can nonetheless be found guilty and thus blameworthy. (Mincing no words in a letter to *Newsweek* a few months after his trial, John Hinckley—a commentator of some personal interest, but still with a point—called the idea "atrocious," for "we would still be in the sorry position of wanting to punish a mentally ill person for his sickness.") A proposal for a verdict of "guilty but insane" would go a step further than "guilty but mentally ill." The option might accurately reflect the gut feelings of a jury— and President Reagan, who endorsed it in an interview with the *Washington Post* on the second anniversary of the shooting—but it would also mean that the jury could convict a defendant whose insanity deprived him of the specific intent necessary to commit a crime, in a contradiction in terms. For a jury that cannot rule with confidence that a defendant was sane, both "guilty but mentally ill" and "guilty but insane" permit the evasion of the hard, unqualified choice between guilty or not guilty usually required by the criminal law.

Eight states allowed the intermediate finding of "guilty but mentally ill" when Hinckley was acquitted in the District of Columbia. Of the states that considered revising their insanity defense laws during 1981 and after—roughly two-thirds—a number debated the merits of this verdict and four adopted it. (One of those, Connecticut, soon repealed its new law.) The Michigan legislature passed the first such law in the country in 1975, to "circumvent" a state court ruling that prompted the release of sixty-four insanity acquittees whom hospitals no longer called dangerous. Two of them committed violent and well-publicized crimes soon after. ("KILLER, FREED AS SANE, HELD IN WIFE'S SLAYING," the *Detroit Free Press* blared in a headline about one.) Michigan lawmakers assumed that their new category would reduce the number of insanity acquittals.

According to a study for the University of Michigan *Journal of Law Reform,* they were wrong. The new group of guilty-but-mentally-ill defendants has been drawn from those previously found guilty and "the new verdict has completely failed in its intended purpose." In the four years before the state adopted the new test as an alternative to verdicts of guilty, not guilty, or not guilty by reason of insanity, an average of .025 percent of the men arrested in Michigan each year (one-fortieth of one percent, or twenty-five out of 100,000) were found not guilty by reason of insanity, for an annual average of fifty-nine acquittees. From 1976, the first full year that the new standard was available, until 1982, the average was virtually identical (.026) and the proportion of defendants found not guilty by reason of insanity out of those raising the defense stayed relatively constant and low, ranging from 8.4 percent in 1977 to five percent in 1981. The study supports the claim of many critics that guilty but mentally ill is a small, compromised, and ineffective reform, and an enemy of more substantial ones.

The most controversial of the Congressional proposals, made in several bills, was restriction of the insanity defense to the *mens rea* (criminal-intent or -mind) standard, which Montana adopted two years before John Hinckley's assassination attempt, Idaho, soon after his acquittal, and Utah, the next year. Supporters and critics alike have called adoption of the test tantamount to abolishing the defense. Designed to reduce the number of insanity acquittees and the range of issues that defendants can raise in an insanity trial, the *mens rea* standard limits psychiatric testimony to comment on the defendant's "intent to commit a crime," a phrase with layers of legal meaning. Insanity is no longer a special defense but, like intoxication or epilepsy, can be raised in the course of a normal criminal trial where the prosecution must ordinarily show the defendant meant to do what he did.

If, for example, a paranoid schizophrenic stole a radio, knowing his deed was against the law yet deluded into believing the box was the only one in the world through which the F.B.I. would broadcast the whereabouts of his enemies, he could be convicted under the law. He intended to do the prohibited act—stealing the radio; no matter why he did it, his specific intent, or *mens rea,* is enough to convict him. Some supporters of the *mens rea* test believe too many insanity defendants either fake mental illness or don't suffer from a serious enough mental disease or defect to absolve them from guilt. But key samples indicate they are wrong. In a study of Erie County, New York, between 1970 and 1980, Henry Steadman and his colleagues found that half of the offenders hospitalized after successful insanity pleas were diagnosed as psychotic schizophrenics, who were seriously ill indeed; about one-seventh had personality disorders, as the government contended Hinckley had at the time of the shooting, and the rest spanned a range from psychotic organic brain syndrome (a mental state brought on by a physiological problem), through alcohol psychosis and drug dependence, to no mental disorder.

The most famous supporter of the *mens rea* test was President Richard Nixon. In 1970, when a bill substituting that standard for the insanity defense was pending in Congress, he called it "the most significant feature of [his] Administration's proposed criminal code," and liked it, he maintained, because it would close the "loophole" of the insanity defense. When the Senate Judiciary Committee issued a written report in 1977 on criminal justice, it attributed to the *mens rea* standard the virtues of fairness and simplicity.

The test can also raise the potential use of the diminished-capacity standard, which allows a jury to find that a defendant's mental disorder deprived him of malice, making him blameless for murder, for example, but responsible on a lesser charge. (Under California's diminished-capacity standard, former San Francisco Supervisor Dan White was convicted of manslaughter instead of murder after he killed Mayor George Moscone and Supervisor Harvey Milk in November of 1978. After resigning his post as supervisor, White had quickly recanted, but the mayor, with Milk's backing, refused to reappoint him. In apparent retaliation, White shot them. At trial, using what became known as the "Twinkies" defense, doctors testified that White's capacity to murder was diminished because he had been under financial and emotional pressure that was aggravated by eating junk food. In the course of White's five-year-and-five-week prison term, the California legislature eliminated the diminished-capacity standard, and a state referendum on victims' rights ratified the step.) Under both *mens rea* and the diminished-capacity standard, the defendant's mental illness at the time of his crime could also be raised at sentencing as a mitigating factor, while his continuing dangerousness could cause his sentence to be increased.

A few days before Hinckley's attempt on the life of President Reagan, as part of the New Right's attack on "social" issues, the *Congressional Record* published an entry by Senator Orrin Hatch, Republican of Utah, about his proposal to replace the insanity defense with a *mens rea* test. Without citing any statistics or detailed analyses on the insanity defense, Hatch contended, first, that "individuals suffering the most serious forms of mental disabilities are unlikely to be criminally convicted under any circumstance"; second, that "the concept of [mental] illness has expanded steadily in this century at the expense of the concept of moral responsibility"; third, that the proposed test would allow courts to face squarely the proper treatment of "the underlying mental problem"; fourth, that it would "encourage more effective use of professional psychiatric resources"; fifth, that "the treatment of those labeled 'mentally ill' as being responsible for their conduct is fully consistent with modern trends in psychiatry to treat such individuals, in most circumstances, as being responsible for their own actions rather than as helpless invalids, buffeted everywhere by circumstances outside of their control"; and sixth, that general insanity rulings have "undermined significantly public respect for and confidence in the criminal justice system as they have resulted in the release of large numbers of individuals clearly dangerous to society."

Senator Hatch's *mens rea* test grew from being a controversial proposal to a commanding one when Attorney General William French Smith gave it the Adminstration's seal of approval immediately after the Hinckley verdict and proposed a similar bill. The Attorney General told the Senate Judiciary Committee that "the criminal-justice system has tilted too decidedly in favor of the rights of criminals and against the rights of society." The Administration's bill, he went on, was designed to "effectively eliminate the insanity defense except in those rare cases in which the defendant lacked the state of mind required as an element of the offense"—thus restoring the balance between "the forces of law and the forces of lawlessness." "A mental disease or defect would be no defense if a defendant knew he was shooting at a human being to kill him," he continued. "Mental disease or defect would constitute a defense only if the defendant did not even know he had a gun in his hand or thought, for example, that he was shooting at a tree." The Attorney General's position departed abruptly from a recommendation made to him a year earlier by his task force on violent crime. The task force had backed the more moderate reform of an optional federal verdict of guilty but mentally ill and civil-commitment power for federal judges, so they would not have to rely on state courts to commit federal defendants found not guilty by reason of insanity. The task force made no comment about a *mens rea* alternative.

On the day before Attorney General Smith threw the Administration's weight behind abolition of the insanity defense, another Justice Department official published a forecast that challenged the position of the abolitionists. They had claimed that the end of the death penalty turned the insanity defense into an anachronism, because, without the threat of death as a penalty for crimes, there was no reason to protect offenders whose responsibility was in question from unduly harsh punishment. Since eight men were executed between 1976, after the Supreme Court reinstituted the death penalty, and 1982, the year of the Hinckley verdict, the claim rested on a dubious foundation. And, in an annual report on death-row populations, Benjamin Renshaw, the acting director of the Bureau of Justice Statistics, predicted, "The United States will witness a spate of executions beginning in 1983–84 without parallel in this nation since the Depression era." Events proved Mr. Renshaw's forecast accurate. In 1983, there were five executions, more than in any year since 1965; of nearly thirteen hundred prisoners on death row, several dozen approached the final stage of appeal, and the Supreme Court repeatedly instructed lower courts not to abide delaying tactics. Putting aside the merits of the Attorney General's contention that abolition of the insanity defense would increase public safety, these facts brought into focus his choice between values implied by the death penalty and by the insanity defense.

Politics aside, support for the *mens rea* standard rested on three assumptions, each of them questionable. First, supporters believed that a *mens rea* test would reduce the number of insanity acquittals. Alan Dershowitz, a professor at the Harvard Law School, disagreed. "In the last analysis," he wrote not long ago, "it is the jury that decides whether an accused is to be convicted or acquitted. No matter how the law reads, it is a deeply entrenched human feeling that those who are grossly disturbed—whether they are called 'madmen,' 'lunatics,' 'insane,' or 'mentally ill'—should not be punished like ordinary criminals. This feeling, which is as old as recorded history, is unlikely to be rooted out by new legislation." Stanley Harris, a federal trial judge who recently served as U.S. Attorney for the District of Columbia and who, as U.S. Attorney, was the prosecutor to whom government lawyers reported in the Hinckley case, was, still earlier, a judge on the District's appeals court. As a member of that bench, he expressed the same view as Dershowitz, but for different reasons. Harris voiced his concern about *mens rea* and diminished-capacity standards in a 1976 opinion about excluding psychiatric testimony on specific intent. In his view, those standards would be ineffectual; they would eliminate the insanity defense and special hearings, while expanding a similar defense within normal criminal trials. For every insanity defense excluded, a diminished-capacity defense would be included. Apart from procedural issues raised by Dershowitz and Harris, supporters of the *mens rea* law were also wrong about basic facts—they believed that an overwhelming number of defendants successfully pleaded insanity each year, instead of thousands; and that insanity acquittees roamed the streets, repeating their crimes against strangers, even though insane offenders, like other assailants, had usually attacked people they knew well (if they attacked anyone) and then gone to mental hospitals from which they departed after a longer term and with a lower rate of repeated wrongdoing than felons.

Second, supporters of a *mens rea* test believed it would lead to better disposition of defendants after trial, whether they were acquitted or convicted. In theory, the acquitted mentally ill would be treated at hospitals or, if dangerous, at hospital units of prisons, and the guilty would go to prisons, where they might also be treated. In practice, argued criminologists and psychiatrists, including Park Dietz, mentally ill offenders in hospitals and prisons rarely receive proper treatment, so that the promise of such treatment for defendants under a *mens rea* test was at least suspect and, probably, false. The *Journal of Law Reform* judged that three-fourths of the people found guilty but mentally ill in

Michigan received no treatment after conviction, and half of the remainder were only occasionally examined. The journal concluded, "As a practical matter, the GBMI [guilty but mentally ill] prisoner is not more likely to receive mental health treatment than the prisoner with a simple guilty verdict; the GBMI prisoner in Michigan is tested and evaluated like any other prisoner." There is no apparent reason to believe a defendant convicted under a *mens rea* test would be handled differently. Disposition of defendants after trial is a troubling issue; debate about mental-health reform might sensibly begin by observing the similarities between hospitals and prisons as instruments of social control. But application of the *mens rea* test hardly assures reform of the mental-health system, or even reform to accomplish the ends described by Senator Hatch and those who agreed with him.

Third, and most important, supporters of the *mens rea* test assumed that the standard drew a distinction appropriate to criminal law. Norval Morris summed up this view in a law-review article in 1968: "It ... seems to me that, within the area of criminal responsibility and psychological disturbance, all that we need is already achieved with existing, long-established rules of intent and crime; I would allow either sane or insane *mens rea* to suffice for guilt."

Sanford Kadish, a professor at the University of California School of Law, Boalt Hall, disagreed, responding that the *mens rea* test requires conviction of "a class of persons who, on any common-sense notion of justice, are beyond blaming and ought not to be punished." Richard Bonnie, a professor at the University of Virginia law school who, after the Hinckley verdict, championed a modern version of the M'Naghten rule to the American Bar Association, to the American Psychiatric Association, and on Capitol Hill, warned, "If the insanity defense is abolished, the law would not take adequate account of the incapacitating effect of severe mental illness."

Many have observed, further, that abolishing the insanity defense would mean abandoning the idea on which the Anglo-American system of criminal justice rests—that of man as a responsible agent with free will—and removing an important distinction between illness and evil. Anticipating Attorney General Smith's view that the *mens rea* test draws an appropriate line by eliminating the murky questions about motivation that crop up in insanity cases, Herbert Packer of Stanford Law School, in a landmark study on *The Limits of the Criminal Sanction* published in 1968, contended that the argument is a red herring: "The insanity defense is not implied or intrinsic to the complex of mental element defenses that make up most of the law of culpability. It is an overriding, *sui generis* defense that is concerned not with what the actor did or believed but with what kind of person he is." The views of Morris, on the one hand, and Kadish, Bonnie, and Packer, on the other, present an obscure but fundamental clash in debate on the *mens rea* test.

Attorney General Smith's testimony on the proposed standard set debate at a more basic level. Mentioning John Hinckley's case only once by name, he implied that it was a typical one. The Attorney General testified: "It is small wonder that trials involving an insanity plea are arduous, expensive and worst of all confusing to the jury. Indeed, the disagreement of the supposed experts is perhaps so basic that it makes the jury's decision rationally impossible." Mr. Smith did not note that most insanity cases were resolved by agreement out of court between prosecutors and defense attorneys, or that many such cases were tried before judges, without juries. (In Washington, D.C., from 1979 through 1983, twenty-four of twenty-six local insanity acquittals were uncontested, and all of them were affirmed by a judge sitting alone. In Michigan, among insanity acquittees in 1982, thirty-six were tried by a judge and only four by a jury.) Peppering his remarks with references to the "illogical choice between competing psychiatric opinions," and "confusing psychiatric testimony," he suggested that the exaggerated circumstances of the Hinckley case are quite common for psychiatrists in the courtroom, and seemed to question the professionalism of doctors who serve as experts in court. Yet even the standard that Smith advocated could not deter a battle of the experts. In the states using the *mens rea* test, the front merely shifted from old issues related to insanity to hoarier ones bound up with intent. Psychiatrist Loren Roth, representing the American Psychiatric Association, told a Congressional committee that the problem of defining intent was "even more ambiguous than applying the insanity standards."

The Attorney General's decision to favor the perceived rights of society over the rights of individuals was most important because it seemed to have wide public support. Before the Hinckley trial, according to a Roper survey, over half of a nationwide sample called permissiveness in the courts and a letdown in moral values major causes of the country's problems. After disbelief, bewilderment, and wonder, outrage followed closely in the wake of the verdict. The American people saw John Hinckley shoot Ronald Reagan and three others over and over again on television, and reports on James Brady's courageous efforts to regain his health did little to quiet the urge for vengeance. If Hinckley had been lynched soon after the shooting it would probably have caused no more anguish to society than his acquittal. According to a poll by ABC News the day after the verdict, eighty-three percent of their national sample thought justice was not done in the Hinckley trial. Many people expressed their hostilities in letters to Judge Parker.

A year later he wrote in the *Washington Post,* "An appreciable amount of the correspondence was regrettably gross, insulting and blatantly racial. The 'black judge'—the 'all black jury' (all but one), and the location of the trial in a 'black city' were all tied to 'blacks' known dislike and hatred of Reagan.' "

Hinckley's insanity acquittal became a symbol of the rise of violent crime and, by extension, of the need to stem that tide. (Dr. Roth testified, "We have a technical term in psychiatry that we use to describe such thinking. It's called displacement. Thus, some of our anger about the insanity defense . . . is displacement, or pushing our concerns about the failure of the whole criminal justice system into the insanity defense.") The causes of crime are complex, but the campaign for abolishing the insanity defense with a *mens rea* test seemed to play on feelings of vengeance and fear in order to win support for an over-simple solution. Aside from retribution, the accepted purposes of punishment— deterrence, rehabilitation, and public protection—seemed to be less important to the campaign than making a statement about the moral force of law. The message was that under the proposed test, only the most insane—men and women who are nothing like us—would escape blame.

Yet questions arose: Would the moral force of the law be enhanced by adoption of a *mens rea* test? Who would be deterred from crime by abolishing the insanity defense? For most of society, the move might strengthen the resolve to obey the law. In a paradox Emile Durkheim observed: "Punishment is above all designed to act upon upright people." Those who saw John Hinckley as a victim of nothing more serious than suburban affluence might gain new respect for the law if it increased its scrutiny of psychological excuses. But those people who would plead insanity are not likely to refrain from crime because the defense no longer exists. Even if they were told explicitly that the defense had been abolished, they would not be likely to make a connection between this change in the law and their own fates.

In 1983, the year after the Attorney General pressed for abolition of the insanity defense, and almost two years after John Hinckley shot the President, the Justice Department quietly retreated from its initial position and endorsed the main parts of a Congressional bill sponsored by John Conyers, Democrat of Michigan, that reflected recommendations from the American Bar Association, the American Psychiatric Association, the American Psychological Association, and the National Mental Health Association, among other groups that proposed reforms of the insanity defense. (Treating the insanity defense as a problem of public policy rather than a matter squarely in its jurisdiction, the American Medical Association called for abolition in 1983. The National Association of Counties followed suit in judging the issue a national one, and, better late than never, formed a fifty-member committee to frame an opinion.) D. Lowell Jensen, who was Assistant Attorney General for the Criminal Division of the Justice Department, made the only official announcement of the Reagan Administration's basic switch in policy, in a footnote to his Congressional testimony.

In the note, he observed "the apparent consensus that has developed for the approach" represented by the Conyers legislation. A bill proposed by Senator Strom Thurmond, Republican of South Carolina, as part of the Senate's omnibus crime law, contained similar features and also earned Administration backing. Both proposed to shift the burden of proof to the defendant in insanity cases, reject the verdict of guilty but mentally ill, and otherwise limit the scope of the insanity defense by making changes in the language of the law that were fervently debated by a small circle of lawyers, doctors, mental-health officials, legislators, and others with a stake in the issue. The bills proposed to restrict the widely used American Law Institute, or Brawner, test by relying only on the cognitive standard (Did he know what he was doing?), dropping the willfulness, or volitional, prong (Could he control his actions?), and adding modifying verbiage to stress that only people who suffered from severe mental problems should qualify.

In effect, the proposed federal law revived the M'Naghten test, still used by sixteen states. Under Conyers, for example, the insanity defense read: "It is a defense to a prosecution for an offense against the United States that, at the time of the conduct alleged to constitute the offense, the defendant suffered from a severely abnormal mental condition that grossly and demonstrably impaired the defendant's perception and understanding of reality and, as a result of that impairment, the defendant did not appreciate the wrongfulness of that conduct." The verdict would also be changed to read "not responsible only by reason of insanity."

In statements supporting their recommendations to Congress to limit the defense, the bar and psychiatric associations generally agreed with each other. The American Bar Association submitted:

> It is just this volitional or behavioral part of the ALI test that has brought the insanity defense under increasing attack. During the 1950s a wave of clinical optimism suggested that scientific knowledge concerning psychopathology had expanded to the extent that informed judgments could be made regarding impairment of behavioral control. That optimism was reflected in the volitional portion of the ALI test. Yet, experience confirms that there is still no accurate scientific basis for measuring one's capacity for self-control or for calibrating the impairment of such capacity. There is, in short, no objective basis for distinguishing between offenders who were

undeterrable and those who were merely undeterred, between the impulse that was irresistible and the impulse not resisted, or between substantial impairment of capacity and some lesser impairment. Whatever the precise terms of the volitional test, the question is unanswerable or, at best, can be answered only by "moral (*and not medical*) guesses." In our opinion, to even ask the volitional question invites fabricated expert claims, undermines the equal administration of the penal law and compromises the law's deterrent effect.

The American Psychiatric Association was more picturesque: "The line between an irresistible impulse, and an impulse not resisted is probably no sharper than between twilight and dusk." In a reference to a number of jury studies, the association declared that "the exact wording of the insanity defense has never, through scientific studies or the case approach, been shown to be the major determinant of whether a defendant is acquitted by reason of insanity," but concluded: "Many psychiatrists . . . believe that psychiatric testimony (particularly of a conclusory nature) about volition is more likely to produce confusion for jurors than is psychiatric testimony relevant to a defendant's appreciation or understanding."

In simple terms, the change in wording proposed by the Conyers and Thurmond bills was designed to put the defense out of the reach of neurotics, like some spouse-killers, who claimed their unconscious overwhelmed their conscience when they attacked. Under this new law, according to the associations that supported it, judges would allow juries the option of an insanity acquittal in fewer cases, and psychiatrists would limit the number of defendants for whom they recommended an insanity plea. The logic of the sponsors was strong enough to overwhelm their sense of reality. Riveted on the fine points of language, they seemed to think juries using their new wording would be made up of philologists, or even lawyers and psychiatrists, who were trained to pick up all shades of meaning. In dissent, the National Mental Health Association advised Congress not to narrow the defense. Through a commission chaired by former senator Birch Bayh, the association maintained: "The problem in the ALI Model Penal Code is not in the volitional element but in placing the burden of proof on the prosecution."

To quiet the popular concern, among psychiatrists as much as among others, that doctors have too much sway in insanity trials, the Conyers and Thurmond bills proposed to prevent them from testifying about the ultimate question before the jury. The draft reform left to the jury the task of reaching a verdict without benefit of doctors' opinions about the defendant's sanity, but permitted psychiatrists to answer a full range of questions about the defendant's mental history, diagnosis, and status at the moment of the act for which he was being tried. Assuming that doctors can contribute to fact-finding as other experts do, the reform was designed to change the process more than the outcome of insanity trials. In brief hearings especially, lawyers sometimes settle for a terse judgment from a psychiatrist on the ultimate question, instead of prompting a witness to give the kind of full description of a defendant's mental state that helps jurors decide about his sanity. Many psychiatrists are vehement about the need for this reform. Alluding to the gap between medical diagnosis and legal judgment, Loren Roth admonished: "The law should not ask psychiatrists questions they cannot answer." The American Psychiatric Association made a similar point in its formal statement: "We adopt this position because it is clear that psychiatrists are experts in medicine, not law."

In the Hinckley trial, whose notoriety prompted the American Psychiatric Association to deny responsibility for the verdict ("Long before there was psychiatry, there was the insanity defense," began the association's vellum-printed statement), the testimony of doctors on the ultimate question of sanity was negligible compared to their long descriptions of the defendant's condition. Of 7,342 transcript pages from the trial, only twenty-six ("a couple of dozen and a deuce," according to a courthouse clerk) were required to capture all of the answers given by the six doctors who testified to the ultimate question of insanity. In *Law, Psychiatry, and Morality,* Alan Stone wrote, "Everything the A.P.A. [the American Psychiatric Association] has proposed in response to the Hinckley verdict is thoughtful and sensible, and yet I believe it would have made no difference in the outcome of the Hinckley trial."

The bulk of the Conyers and Thurmond bills tackled what happens to an insanity defendant before and after trial. The bills provided for screening, examination, and treatment of people who are incompetent to stand trial, and the Conyers proposal assured them legal hearings if they disagreed with a clinic's ruling about their competence. Like the Thurmond bill, the Conyers submission also established, for the first time, federal commitment procedures for people found not guilty by reason of insanity in federal courts; to date, these courts have relied on state agencies to take responsibility for the handful of federal insanity acquittees, in addition to their own. In a few federal cases, like the 1983 insanity acquittal of a wealthy, toupee-topped Seattle man charged with molesting an eight-year-old girl ("SEX-CASE MILLIONAIRE GOES FREE," the city's *Post-Intelligencer* announced), the local prosecutor could not readily commit the offender under state law.

Disposition of defendants after trial is obviously the key element in guarding against repetition of crime by insanity acquittees. As with many insanity-defense-related issues, the subject of commitment triggers its own debate. A recent

Harvard Law Review note began succinctly: "An acquittal by reason of insanity is rarely a ticket to freedom." Most states commit insanity defendants more easily than civil patients. No one argues that society should not be protected from defendants who continue to be dangerous after trial, and in most states, the *Law Review* observes, the assumption—which includes an element of retribution—is that "a person who commits a crime is either responsible enough to deserve punishment, or insane enough to deserve commitment."

Opinions vary about procedures, standards, and responsibilities for commitment and release. An increasingly common approach in the states is to commit and evaluate a defendant for fifty days after acquittal, after which he may be released or committed for a long term. This practice provides a safeguard against the immediate discharge of dangerous offenders and, on the other hand, the extended detention of relatively harmless offenders—a coat thief or a small-time forger, for example—who were acquitted by reason of insanity. Standards for release also vary. A standard requiring that a defendant be certified "cured" means that someone who suffers from a mental illness like schizophrenia, which can defy cure, is not likely to be released. A standard of "no longer dangerous" depends on too-often unreliable prediction, but allows the chronically-ill offender to be released if his leaning toward crime seems controllable through drugs and outpatient treatment. Whatever the standard, the current vogue is for judges or panels like parole boards to make independent decisions on release of defendants, rather than to rubber-stamp hospital recommendations. It is important to recognize that adequate commitment procedures can be addressed and managed separately from the merits of the insanity defense.

The subject of commitment raises another issue that

provokes sharp dispute: the appropriate length of treatment for an insanity acquittee. In 1963, two professors at Yale Law School proposed to abolish the insanity defense and end the hypocrisy of exculpating offenders and then sentencing them to indeterminate periods at hospitals that were worse than prisons. Today, the view that ties commitment to punishment argues that offenders should either stay in hospitals for as long as they would have served in prison, or finish out their prison terms once hospitals release them. For crimes that carry protracted sentences, this policy would assure quarantine of sick offenders. But what about the coat thief and the forger? Should they be released from the hospital after periods equal to the brief prison sentences they would otherwise receive? No, decided the Supreme Court, a year after the Hinckley verdict, in Jones *v*. United States, which considered the case of a man who was arrested while trying to steal a jacket and whose insanity plea was accepted without contest by the government. Four justices dissented. Represented by Justice Lewis Powell's opinion, the majority of five ruled that insanity acquittees "constitute a special class that should be treated differently." The justices held that an insanity acquittal implies a finding of criminal conduct, which indicates dangerousness, and "supports an inference of continuing mental illness." They concluded about the defendant, "The purpose of his commitment following an insanity acquittal is to treat the individual's mental illness and protect him and society from his potential dangerousness. . . . There simply is no necessary correlation between the severity of the offense and length of time necessary for recovery."

Epilogue

IF JOHN HINCKLEY had not been acquitted by reason of insanity, the defense would probably have remained a fascinating and popularly neglected topic in the law. In the heat of the summer following the Hinckley verdict and in the years after, Attorney General William French Smith did not comment on reports about the decision that inadvertently sparked wide interest in the defense. In May and again in November of 1981, John Hinckley had offered to plead guilty to all counts against him, in exchange for a recommendation by the Justice Department that his sentences be served concurrently, not consecutively, so that he might be eligible for parole in fifteen years rather than serving in prison for life. According to the law in Washington, D.C., under which Hinckley was committed to St. Elizabeths, after a finding of not guilty by reason of insanity a defendant must be released from the hospital if he can prove he is no longer dangerous, as a result of mental illness, to himself or society. The upshot of the Hinckley verdict was that he can be released from St. Elizabeths long before he would have been eligible for parole under the terms of the plea he offered, even though his early release would be sure to spark bitter controversy.

The Justice Department wanted to win the Hinckley case in a show trial and put the defendant away for life; the department viewed plea bargaining with the man who tried to assassinate the President as unseemly, improper, and wrong, and believed that his willingness to plead guilty cast doubt on his insanity defense. But Hinckley's unexpected victory became a spur for reform and, in light of the unaccepted pleas, the verdict turned into a sacrifice accepted by the government for the sake of limiting, if not abolishing, the insanity defense.

In the two years after the verdict half the states enacted cutbacks in the defense, so the government's momentary defeat at law yielded an enduring change in justice. In 1984, by a vote of ninety-one to one, the Senate followed suit and adopted a 387-page criminal-justice bill that contained an insanity defense modeled on Senator Thurmond's proposal and the 141-year-old M'Naghten rule. Urging the House of Representatives to join the Senate in passing the new law—the first federal statute on the plea—President Reagan called it "the most comprehensive anti-crime legislation in more than a decade." The bill was designed to reduce violent crime, and the insanity defense was one of the measure's heralded provisions. Favor for the reform still rested on ideology more than fact. So did opposition. The Senate voted enthusiastically to protect society by limiting the insanity defense. When the Democrat-led House refused to vote on the measure early in the Presidential campaign and thus give candidate Reagan a victory, Attorney General Smith said about Washington, "Here you get to the merits only as a poor third. First you have to get through perception. Then there's a layer of politics. You may finally reach the merits, but very often decisions are made on the basis of perception and politics only."

The senators accepted that their choice was between the forces of law and the forces of lawlessness, as posed by Mr. Smith. In final discussion of the bill, none of them looked behind the veil of the dichotomy presented. Reform of the insanity defense had become a surrogate for resolution of the most profound issues in criminal justice, and, between polar views about crime, punishment, and responsibility, the Republican-led senators chose to emphasize retribution. They may have gained the satisfaction of grappling with a large issue. They may also have taken out on a narrow legal problem the frustrations citizens feel with a disorderly, unmanageable, and daunting system, and, by voting to cut back the insanity defense, shown a willingness to give up a civilized standard for a harsh reminder of the balance of power between the individual and society.

Acknowledgments

For encouragement or teaching, I am grateful to Robert Coles, Robert Coulam, Richard Dey, Robert Fitzgerald, Father James Harold Flye, John Gardner, Jamie Gorelick, Charles House, Michael Ignatieff, David Ignatius, David Jackson, Charles and Fern Nesson, Andrew Nighswander, Martin and Anne Peretz, Jay Reich, Raphael Sagalyn, Patti Saris, Arthur Segel, and Leonard Zax, and, in memory, Robert Bingham, Elizabeth Bishop, and Richard and Katharine Day. On this project, in particular, Robert Shapiro, Richard Waldhorn, and William Yeomans gave thoughtful advice, as readers and friends.

Joyce Bouvier typed the early drafts of my manuscript, and Leslie Zupan, one of the last. James Polk of NBC News shared with me fruits of his reporting on the Butner papers. George Gibson, David Godine, William Goodman, Sarah Saint-Onge, and Dorothy Straight showed enthusiasm and skill in helping to make this essay into a book. At *The New Yorker,* Tony Gibbs and Lillian Ross provided welcome guidance and a sense of camaraderie, and others of the magazine's editorial and checking departments, Richard Sacks above all, improved my work. For his generous backing and counsel, I am especially grateful to the magazine's editor, William Shawn.

I couldn't mention in my writing all of the people who played substantial parts in the events I covered or in the wide debate triggered by John Hinckley. I want to highlight the roles of Judith Miller and Lon Babby, who assisted Vincent Fuller and Gregory Craig as counsel for the defense, and of Robert Chapman, Marc Tucker, and Constance Belfiore, who teamed with prosecutor Roger Adelman.

Finally, I thank my family for strong and constant support and, for her faith and love, my wife, Susan, to whom this book is dedicated.

Index

Adams, Rufus, 50–58, 93–95
Adelman, Roger, 8–9, 89–90, 100
American Bar Association, 118, 119–120
"American Front" newsletter, 36
American Law Institute (ALI) test. *See* Brawner rule
American Psychiatric Association, 64, 116, 118, 120, 121–122
Asinof, Eliot, 43

Bayh, Birch, 121
Bazelon, David, 21–23, 29, 73
Bear, David, 75–84, 89
Benchley, Nathaniel, 78
Benjamin, Darrell, 37
Blyther, George, 102
Bonnie, Richard, 114–115
Brady, James, 8, 89, 116
Brawner, Archie, 24
Brawner rule, 24, 28, 49, 119–121
Bremer, Arthur, 88

Brown, Nathalia, 102
Burger, Warren, 30

Capital punishment, 111–112
Carpenter, William, 66–68, 73, 89
Carter, Jimmy, 7, 38
Catcher in the Rye, The (Salinger), 43
CAT-scan evidence, 79–85
Cavanaugh, James, 87
Chapman, Mark David, 40
Cheeks, Cecil J., 53–54
Chicago Daily News, 31
Coffey, Lawrence, 102
Commitment, 93–95, 123–124, 125–126
  See also Hospitalization
Congressional Record, 110
Conyers, John, 118, 119
Conyers bill, 118, 119, 120, 121, 122
Copelin, Maryland, 102
Country Style, 36
Craig, Gregory, 92, 99

Crime statistics, 25
*Criminal Violence, Criminal
Justice* (Silberman), 4

Darrow, Clarence, 31
Death penalty, 111–112
Delahanty, Thomas, 8, 89
De Niro, Robert, 76, 89
Dershowitz, Alan, 112
Devlin, Lord, 29
*Diagnostic and Statistical
Manual of Mental Disorders*
(DSM-III), 64–65
Dietz, Park, 68–73, 75, 90, 91,
113
Displacement, 117
Drake, Belinda, 102
Drummond, Edward, 19
Durham, Monte, 21
Durham rule, 21–24
Durkheim, Emile, 117

Esquire, 42
Evans, Dorothy, 54
Exclusionary rule, 4

Fan, The (Randall), 43, 78
FitzGerald, Frances, 42
Ford, Gerald, 32
Forensic psychiatrists, testimony
of, 63–73, 75–90
Foster, Jodie, 10, 17, 36
Hinckley's obsession with, 38,
39, 40, 41, 42, 43, 72, 76–
77, 78, 91
Hinckley's phone conversation
with, 16, 38
Hinckley's threats against, 16,
39, 67, 68
Hinckley's writings and, 11–
12, 38, 40, 41, 43, 47, 90
in *Taxi Driver,* 77, 89

testimony of, 15–16
treatment of Hinckley, 16
Fox is Crazy Too, The (Asinof),
43, 78
Fuller, Vincent, 10, 90–92

Garfield, James, 20
Garner, Alfreda, 51, 52, 55
Goldman, Thomas, 86–87, 89
Goldstein, Abraham, 25, 28–29
Gordon, Steven, 51, 52, 55, 95
"Guilty but mentally ill" verdict,
106–108, 114
Guiteau, Charles, 20–21

Harris, Stanley, 112–113
Harvard Law Review, 123
Hatch, Orrin, 110
Helms, Richard, 12
Hinckley, Diane, 14–15, 34, 37,
38, 39
Hinckley, JoAnn Moore:
on Hinckley as child, 33
on Hinckley's suicide attempt,
39
marriage of, 65
and son, 39, 40, 41, 43, 65–66
testimony of, 12–13, 14
at verdict, 99, 100
Hinckley, John W., Jr.:
account of shooting, 60
anxiety attacks of, 36, 37
appearance at trial, 9–10, 88,
91–92
commitment of, 100, 125
drugs taken by, 36, 37, 39, 42,
43, 76, 77, 83
early arrest of, 39
fantasies of, 10, 11–12, 35,
39, 41, 77–78, 91
following Jimmy Carter, 7–8,
38

Hinckley, John W., Jr. (*cont.*)
  following Ronald Reagan, 40,
    41–42
  guns of, 35, 36, 37, 38, 39, 40,
    41, 42, 76–77
  history of, 33–47
  on insanity defense, 106
  I.Q. of, 85
  letter to Jodie Foster, 11–12,
    90
  mental state of, 17, 36, 37, 38,
    66–73, 75–92
  parents' treatment of, 13–14,
    34–35, 37, 41
  question of feigned insanity, 78–
    79, 86
  reaction to family at trial, 14–
    15
  reaction to Jodie Foster's
    testimony, 15–16
  shooting of Ronald Reagan, 8–
    9, 60
  suicide attempts of, 39, 40, 65,
    83
  therapy of, 10, 13, 39, 40, 41,
    65–66
  at verdict, 99–101
  writings of, 11–12, 34, 43–47,
    60
Hinckley, John W., Sr. (Jack):
  business of, 33–34, 62
  marriage of, 65
  and son, 40, 41, 43, 65–66
  testimony of, 13–14
  at verdict, 99, 100
Hinckley, Scott, 15, 34
Hinckley trial:
  CAT-scan evidence, 79–85
  costs, 59–62
  final arguments, 89–92
  Foster's testimony, 15–16
  Hinckley's appearance, 9–10
  instructions to jury, 97–98,
    102, 106
  jury, 98–99, 102

opening of, 7
  parents' testimony, 13–14
  psychiatrists' testimony, 65–
    73, 75–88
  public opinion following
    verdict, 116–117
  tapes of Hinckley, 16–17
  Taxi Driver showing, 88–89
  verdict, 97–100, 125–126
Hopper, John:
  recommendations to parents,
    10, 13, 91
  testimony of, 65–66
  treatment of Hinckley, 10, 34,
    36, 39, 40, 41, 43, 65–66,
    70, 90, 91
Hospitalization, 26–27, 93–95,
  104, 123–124, 125–126
Hubbard, David G., 43

Insanity defense:
  acquittals based on, 27, 55–
    56, 102–103, 104, 107–108,
    115–116
  in Adams trial, 50–58, 93–95
  arguments against, 3–4, 26, 29–
    31, 102–104
  Brawner rule and, 24, 49, 119–
    121
  burden of proof in, 105–106
  commitment and release under,
    123–124, 125–126
  Congress and, 104–105, 118–
    122, 126–127
  death penalty and, 111–112
  in District of Columbia, 49–
    58, 105–106
  DSM-III and, 64–65
  Durham rule and, 21–24
  and "guilty but mentally ill"
    verdict, 106–108, 114
  history of, 19–32
  M'Naghten rule and, 20, 22,
    119

Insanity defense (*cont.*)
 mens rea test and, 30, 108–117
 public opinion and, 116–117
 recidivism following acquittals, 104
 reform of, 104–105, 118–122, 126–127
 statistics on, 27, 55–56, 102–103, 107–108, 115–116
 See also Hinckley trial
Insanity Defense, The (Goldstein), 28
Insanity Defense Reform Act, 27

Jackson, Andrew, 31
Jensen, D. Lowell, 118
Johnson, Sally, 87–89, 90, 91
Johnson, Tonya, 53
Jones *v.* United States, 124
Journal of Law Reform, 107–108, 113–114
Jury, 98–99, 102
 instructions to, 97–98, 102, 106

Kadish, Sanford, 114
Kennedy, Robert F., 31
King, Martin Luther, Jr., 32
Kohlman, Gary, 51, 52, 55, 56–58, 94–95

Law, Psychiatry, and Morality (Stone), 122
Lawrence, Richard, 31
Lennon, John, 10, 16, 17, 32, 40, 42, 44–45
Leopold, Nathan, Jr., 31
Limits of the Criminal Sanction, The (Packer), 115
Loeb, Richard, 31

McCarthy, Timothy, 9
M'Naghten, Daniel, 19
M'Naghten rule, 20, 22, 119
Meese, Edwin, 3, 103, 105
Mens rea test, 30, 108–117
Milk, Harvey, 109
Minnesota Multiphasic Personality Inventory, 85–86
Monahan, John, 28
Morris, Norval, 29–30, 114
Moscone, George, 109
Moultrie, Carl, 51, 52, 93, 94, 95

Nation, The, 36
National Socialist Party, 35, 38
Newsweek, 106
New York Herald, 21
Nixon, Richard, 109

Ono, Yoko, 16
Oswald, Lee Harvey, 88

Packer, Herbert, 115
Parker, Barrington, 7, 52, 66, 92, 99
 background of, 12
 on CAT-scan evidence, 79, 81–85
 instructions to jury, 97–98, 102, 106
 public opinion on, 116–117
Peel, Robert, 19
People, 36
Powell, Lewis, 124
Prelinger, Ernst, 85–86, 89
President's Commission on Crime in the District of Columbia, 105
Psychiatry:
 and cure for violence, 28
 and law, 63–92

Psychiatry (*cont.*)
  and treatment of mental
    illness, 26–27
Public Defender Service, 49, 55–
  56

Randall, Bob, 43
Rappeport, Jonas, 87
Ray, Isaac, 22
Ray, James Earl, 88
Reagan, Ronald:
  followed by Hinckley, 40, 41–
    42
  Hinckley's letter to Jodie
    Foster on, 11–12
  on insanity defense, 105, 106,
    126
  shooting of, 8–9, 42
Rector, Milton, 27
Renshaw, Benjamin, 112
Rodin, Ernst, 87
Romeo and Juliet, 43, 78
Roosevelt, Theodore, 31
Roth, Loren, 116, 117, 121

St. Elizabeths Hospital, 93–95,
  98, 100, 125
Salinger, J. D., 43
Schizophrenia, 76
  CAT-scan in diagnosis of, 79–
    85
Seattle Post-Intelligencer, 122
Shapiro, A. David, 54–55
Silberman, Charles, 4
Simon, Rita James, 23
Sims, Chris, 34
Sims, Steve, 34
Sirhan, Sirhan, 88
Sirica, John, 82

Skyjacker, The (Hubbard), 43
Smith, William French, 3, 111–
  112, 115–116, 125, 126
Soldier of Fortune, 60
Specter, Arlen, 102, 105
Steadman, Henry, 28, 102–104
Stone, Alan, 4, 25–27, 28, 122

Taxi Driver, 10, 35, 43, 76–78,
  88–89
Thurmond, Strom, 118, 126
Thurmond bill, 118, 120, 121,
  122
Traylor, William, 51, 52
"Twinkies" defense, 109–110

U. S. Supreme Court:
  on Durham rule, 23
  on length of commitment, 124

Vanderbilt Energy Corporation,
  34, 62
Voir dire, 50–51

Wallace, George, 32
Washington Post, 21, 98, 102,
  117
Washington Star, 41
Washington *v.* United States, 83
Wechsler Adult Intelligence Scale,
  85
Welcome to Xanadu (Benchley),
  78
White, Dan, 109–110
Williams, Edward Bennett, 10
Williams & Connolly, 10, 59, 62

THE INSANITY DEFENSE

has been set by Dix Type Inc., Syracuse, New York, in Sabon, a face designed by Jan Tschichold (1902–1974). In 1960, a committee of German master printers commissioned Tschichold to create a face that could be used interchangeably in hand composition, monotype, and linotype. This difficult assignment was further complicated by the requirement that the new face be based on those designs first cut in the sixteenth century by Claude Garamond.

For inspiration, Tschichold turned to the famous 1592 specimen sheet of Egelnolff-Berner, modeling his roman on Saint Augustine, a face attributed to Garamond, and his italic on a Granjon face. The subsequent type, which, it was hoped, would replace the endless variations of Garamond already on the market, was named after Jacques Sabon, a punchcutter employed at the Egelnolff-Berner typefoundry who eventually purchased the operation and transformed it into one of the great foundries of the sixteenth century.

Printed and bound by The Haddon Craftsmen, Scranton, Pennsylvania.

Typography and binding design by Lisa De Francis.